JOURNEY
TO THE
IMPOSSIBLE

JOURNEY
TO THE
IMPOSSIBLE

Designing an Extraordinary Life

SCOTT JEFFREY

CREATIVE CRAYON PUBLISHING
NEW YORK

Creative Crayon Publishing
1173A Second Avenue #356
New York, New York 10021

Photograph of Scott Jeffrey by Peter Nash
Cover and interior design by David Riley & Associates

First Edition
Printed in the U.S.A.

Library of Congress Catalog Card Number: 2001096040
ISBN 0-9714815-0-4

To my mom, Carrie,
the most amazingly loving soul,
incredible teacher, and best friend
a son could ever want

ACKNOWLEDGEMENTS

I am extremely grateful for the help and support of the following:

First, to God, for blessing me with the incredible gift of life and for divinely guiding me on my own *Journey to the Impossible.*

To my mom, Carrie, and Steve, for their constant support and encouragement throughout my unpredictable and often unexplainable adventures in life.

To Danita Allen, for being the greatest editor on the planet. Not only do you possess wizard-like editing skills, but you are an extraordinary soul as well.

To Eric Katz, for taking the time to tell your story but, more importantly, for being a truly amazing individual and an inspiration to all.

To Ty Mattson, for creating the most *wowing* cover and interior design the world has ever seen.

To Alejandra and Patrick McCurley, for doing such an accurate, fast, and fun final proof of this book.

To Bill Howell, for being a living example of someone who consistently *Creates the Impossible.*

To Zachary Smith, for creating the most awe-inspiring web site, including the one for this book.

To Scott Balaban and Harris Rabin, for always making yourselves available to help with the project.

To Rebecca Marcus, for being a brave soul and taking a first stab at editing this book.

To Peter Nash, for being a masterful photographer.

To John Appuhn, for taking the time to assist me in some non-legal legal matters.

To Kathy O'Hehir, for reviewing this book in such an

impossible time frame.

To Crockette Johnson, for writing *Harold and the Purple Crayon* and providing a powerful symbol of possibility and creation throughout my life.

And finally, and certainly most importantly, to a man who desires zero public acknowledgement for all the indescribable magic he continues to create in the world. Thank you for being an inspiring mentor, a guiding coach, and a loving friend—you are truly extraordinary. This book would not exist if it were not for you. You are a true *Goonie*, the ultimate *Creator of the Impossible*.

TABLE OF CONTENTS

Contents

Note to Fellow Travelers

I find it only fitting to begin our *Journey* together by telling you a little about my personal journey through *impossible* times and explaining why we are on this exciting voyage together.

I had one of those "after-school special" childhoods. Remember those two-hour made-for-TV movies that were fairly painful to watch and always ran right when you got home from school. My story starts with my parents' divorce at age three and a strong, caring, loving mother, and a father who was mentally unfit for everyday life, to put it mildly. What follows is over thirteen years of court trials and custody battles, spanning five judges, twelve shrinks, some violence, and a lot of heartache, crying, and pain.

In the midst of all this, I grew up—a little quicker than most perhaps, since maturing quickly was necessitated by my survival. I don't want to paint a completely black picture here. I still did all the things "normal" kids did at my age: school, summer camp, a wide variety of sporting events, and birthday parties with friends. But behind this projection of normalcy laid a great deal of fear, discomfort, and uncertainty about my future.

Luckily, I was enormously blessed with an incredibly strong, compassionate and loving mom who did everything in her power to make sure I would thrive. I have little doubt I would not have survived so gracefully without her uncompromising support and that of my loving family.

When I turned sixteen, the court decided I was old enough to make my own decision about seeing my father. I chose not to see him, and for the most part, the saga ended there.

Looking back on these experiences more than ten years later, I am filled with a great sense of gratitude and strength, as well as a sense of divine guidance that everything happens to serve a purpose. I don't regret those arduous years of my childhood because they helped shape who I am today. They taught me never to sweat the small stuff, a lesson we all need to relearn over and over again.

For the past ten years, I have been fascinated with understanding our human psychology and development and have aggressively searched for ways to become more, ways to enhance my life and the lives of those around me. During my junior year in college, in a time of great confusion and questioning, I began reading a book a week— a practice I have continued to this day, though nowadays it's more like two or three. The topics have ranged from pop psychology, personal growth, and eastern/western philosophies to business strategy, quantum physics, and health.

Following college, I began devouring this information at an accelerated rate, reading diligently, going to seminars and listening to audiocassette programs. My thirst for knowledge took me through many majestic cities in Western Europe, to the enchanting rain forests of Central America, and on countless retreats and hikes through the magnificent nature of the United States. I wasn't really certain what I was looking for in these places, but I figured I'd have to look in places few people were looking.

Each time I picked up a new book, I thought to myself, "This book could possess the answers I'm looking for." Like a curious child, I read the words of hundreds of brilliant men and women and explored new lands with eager anticipation and excitement. I began applying what I learned in my work and in my daily life, capturing any new lessons, ideas, and experiences in journals and notepads.

There were many times when I questioned what I was doing. Was I growing? Was I really learning anything new? What was different? What was changing? Even in those times of doubt, I felt this mysterious force propelling me forward.

My *Journey* is in no way over. In fact, I sense in many ways, my personal odyssey of discovery has just begun. The transformational process continues even as I write these words. The difference is, I no longer question this process, at least, not as often. I embrace it with all the energy I can muster every single day, knowing full well that today could be my *Journey's* end. And if it is, I will take great comfort in knowing that I have truly lived this day and I have served my purpose.

This book shares some of the important things I've learned thus far—important in the sense that I believe they can help you along your own *Journey* in creating an extraordinary life. I believe very strongly that nothing is *impossible*, which is a common theme throughout this book.

I tell you a little of my childhood experiences, not to sadden or create pity, but rather to highlight and illustrate why I have committed my life to the service of helping others and to discovering effective ways to experience a more extraordinary life. And, in case you are curious, I have since forgiven my father in my heart for what he did and the person he has become.

We each have our own experiences, beliefs, and values that shape our decisions and our actions—the fact that these experiences, beliefs, and values are different for each of us is why we live in such a diverse and rich society.

We all have a story, in fact many stories, but it is what we choose to do with our stories that determines the quality of life we create for ourselves and those we love. Sometimes it is too easy to use our "stories" as excuses to why our lives are not turning out as planned. Beware of this common pitfall and use your past experiences—good

Introduction

or bad—to create a life with your own high personal standards, one that will keep your passion and excitement for living on a glorious ascent.

With that, let us begin.

Happy Journeys!

Scott Jeffrey
New York, NY

The Purple Crayon

Every child is an artist.
The problem is how to remain an artist after growing up.
—Pablo Picasso

The *Journey to the Impossible* starts with a crayon. That's right, a crayon. But not just any ordinary crayon, this extraordinary symbol of creation is purple!

One night, when Harold was a small boy, he decided to go for a walk in the moonlight with his purple crayon. He drew a straight path and continued on the horizon until he was ready for a change. He and his crayon strayed off the path and came to a place where he thought a forest should be. He began to draw a forest but decided to make the forest only one tree so he wouldn't get lost. It was a glorious apple tree. But Harold was afraid

6

people would take his apples so he created a dragon to scare them off. The dragon turned out to be so scary it startled Harold, causing him to unconsciously draw an ocean.

Harold began to sink straight down but he came up thinking fast—he drew himself a boat, a sail boat setting sail on a new voyage. When Harold got tired of the sea, he drew a beach and laid anchor. After having a nice picnic, Harold decided it was time to start heading home. The thing was, now he didn't know where home was. He figured, though, that if he could get up high enough, he'd be able to see his bedroom window. So he began drawing steps to a large mountain, leading him high up in the sky. Once he reached the peak, he looked around but was unable to see a thing.

Harold lost his focus, slipped off the other side of the mountain, where he hadn't yet drawn a descent. Harold plummeted at an accelerating rate, but once again, he came up thinking fast. Harold quickly drew a helium balloon and a basket to stand in. He gained altitude quickly, continuing to look for his home. As Harold began to land, he began drawing different windows, in an attempt to find his own. He went on to draw an entire city, filled with hundreds and hundreds of windows, none of which was his own. In a moment of des-

peration, Harold drew a policeman who only pointed him in the direction he was going.

But then Harold had a profound moment of enlightenment. He remembered that the moon was in a particular place, in the center of his window. He hypothesized that if he could draw his window in the exact position around the moon, he'd at last be in his bedroom. And so he did, relieved to finally be home. Now, Harold, being exhausted from this crazy adventure, drew his bed, drew up his covers, dropped his purple crayon, and went to sleep.

Are you familiar with this story? It's adapted from a classic children's book called, *Harold and the Purple Crayon*, by Crockett Johnson, a text of pure brilliance. It's a book I absolutely loved as a child, but I'm even more fascinated with it now. Harold and the symbol of the *Purple Crayon* personify our *Journey to the Impossible*. The *Purple Crayon* is a symbol of possibility and a reminder that we truly can *create* whatever we want in our lives. Harold is an ideal example of a life strategist who shapes the environment around him.

Whether we're conscious of it or not, we're constantly *creating the world around us*—for better or worse. We *create* through our everyday thought process, our continual line of questions, and our habitual and spontaneous actions. We all have a *purple crayon*, but only a select few choose what to draw. In essence, most of us have neglected our innate ability to create, to build, and to make things happen in every area of our lives.

How do you tap into the power of your *purple crayon*? You start by becoming aware that your magnificent crayon exists within you. Then…begin to draw like a kid. A kid doesn't walk around with preconceived notions about how things are. A kid explores, stays curious, tries new things, and embraces each moment with joy, excitement, and wonder. A kid doesn't worry about how the drawing will look when it's finished. A kid can take his *purple crayon* in hand and draw whatever his heart desires.

Unfortunately, this is not usually true for an adult. An adult hasn't picked up his *crayon* in years, often decades. He has forgotten that his *crayon* is the gateway to making his dreams come true. He no longer spends a great deal of time thinking about what to draw and consequently, he rarely attempts to draw or create anything anymore. As a result, the whole world is worse off.

But here's the wonderful news: your *purple crayon* is still right there. It's been lying dormant for a while, waiting patiently to come out and play. You need only reach inside, take hold, and remember that the creation process always begins with a single thought. Get crystal clear on what you want in your life, pick up your *purple crayon* and begin to draw. And please remember, this is your life we're talking about. Draw outside the lines and have fun!

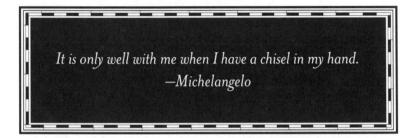

It is only well with me when I have a chisel in my hand.
—Michelangelo

How to Read the Journey

Our *Journey to the Impossible* is going to take us around, over, and through the realm of the unknown as we discover the powerful strategies needed to achieve the *impossible* in every area of our lives. During this odyssey of growth and discovery we will explore what has to happen to get what we want in life. We will blast through ideas encompassing creativity, momentum planning, courage, passion, growth, energy, leadership, communication, relationships, fun, and more.

This *Journey* requires your full attention and an enormous sense of fun because if you don't want to enjoy the process of achieving an extraordinary life, then what's the point? If there's a specific area of focus, concern, or interest within the *Journey* that you strongly want to address now, well, by all means. This book does not need to be read in a linear fashion. Start on the last page. Start in the middle. Read upside down. Whatever works for you. The important thing is that you absorb the information. You could even try going to sleep with the book on your head and hope that osmosis takes over. (The author would like to note he has had little luck with this last suggestion but...you are welcome to give it a shot.)

It's time to take your seat and buckle up—this ride may get bumpy.

But first...

Seeking the Impossible

One of the main weaknesses of mankind is the average man's familiarity with the word "impossible."
—Napoleon Hill

You're reading a book with a title that defies traditional thinking. How can you *Journey to the Impossible*? Many people would be afraid to open a book about dealing with *impossibilities* because they expect any attempt to do the impossible would fail, creating a painful experience—so they don't even try.

I want to start off by debunking this whole notion of "impossibility." The term is used quite frequently in this book to make a powerful point: ***Nothing is impossible***. The notion of *impossibility* is preposterous. It's insane. It's ludicrous. How could someone say something is impossible?

Just because they think they can't do it? Or because no one they know has done it? I get excited every time I hear someone utter the words *impossible, inconceivable, unattainable, unachievable,* or *unfeasible* because I know an adventure is about to begin.

Electricity and the light bulb were an *impossibility.* A human's safe passage through the sky was *unfeasible.* The four-minute mile was simply *unachievable.* But Thomas Edison, the Wright Brothers, and Roger Banister went and did it anyway.

To live an extraordinary life and consistently create what you want, you must become an *Impossibility Seeker*—a *Creator of the Impossible*—those daring few souls who never settle, always striving to become more. As an *Impossibility Seeker,* it is up to you to decide where the *Journey* takes you and what quality of life you want to create. Feel amazingly grateful to have the ability to make such critical decisions, but take care in making them. Your decisions along the *Journey* define your destiny.

Take a deep breath, put on big a smile, and let the Journey to the Impossible *begin...*

> The impossible is happening everyday.
> —Fairy godmother from Cinderella

Journey's Survival Kit

Things to pack on your *Journey* to creating an extraordinary life:

Take a scroll filled with life's timeless treasures,
Take a journal to record the story of your life,
Take a bottle of water to energize your body,
Take a verse of poetry to energize your soul,
Take a compass to always have direction,
Take a match to keep your passion lit, and
Take a map to plot your future course.

Take your courage to overcome adversity,
Take your compassion to connect with another soul,
Take your curiosity to learn something new,
Take your passion to ignite the fire in your heart,
Take your attention to focus on what's most important,

Introduction

Take your strength to help those in need,
Take your creativity to make the world a better place,
Take your thoughts to create what you truly desire, and
Take your love to spread around the world.

And if your survival kit ever happens to get lost, stolen, stepped on, mangled, broken, drowned, or dropped off a cliff, fear not. For all that you need to survive, thrive, and prosper is within you right now. Embrace the *Journey* and love everyday.

Create the Impossible

To stand directly in the face of fear,
To look fear square in the eyes with an attitude that says,
     "Bring it on,"
To smirk at fear, actually intimidating it if only for a moment,
This is what one must do to *create the impossible.*

To burn all bridges of retreat,
To be so crystal clear about what you want that you ache inside,
To have an unconquerable burning desire to build your empire,
This is what one must do to *create the impossible.*

To develop an air of defiance, laughing at the status quo,
To be a dominating force for good, a fortress of creation,
To lead by example, catalyzing a tidal wave of change,
This is what one must do to *create the impossible.*

To have total resolve that solutions always present themselves,
To be open to change, willing to bend and stretch, but never break,
To adapt to living in the unknown, staying focused on your vision,
To anticipate change with an almost clairvoyant accuracy,
This is what one must do to *create the impossible.*

To own it, bring it inside, make it a part of you,
To be relentless in your pursuit to build a magnificent empire,
To be unreasonable in the face of reason,
To dominate, lead, inspire, and grow,
This is what one must do to *create the impossible.*

–Scott Jeffrey

ACHIEVING
IMPOSSIBLE
RESULTS

Create Your Vision

The world makes way for a man who knows where he is going.
—Ralph Waldo Emerson

Clarity creates the *impossible*. Clarity of what you want and where you want to go enables you to divert all of your energy and attention to finding a way. An inspiring vision for the future will guide you on a magnificent *Journey to the Impossible*.

You need a **compelling vision** that moves you in the direction you want to go—the more compelling your vision, the more extraordinary your life. Your vision must encompass all the important components of your life. Your vision statement will project your new lifestyle, your relationships with your loved ones, your career, what you are contributing, who you are becoming, what your life is about, and any other aspects of your life that inspire you.

Make sure your vision is large—larger than you are now. A grand vision has the power to move you toward what you want to create and who you want to become. A small vision will not have the power to move you.

See yourself one year down the road, five years, ten years, and twenty years—see who you are and what your life is about. Your vision statement can guide you to a life that most people would say is...*Impossible.*

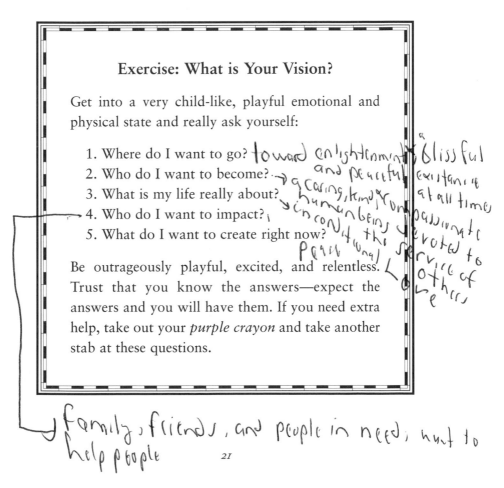

Exercise: What is Your Vision?

Get into a very child-like, playful emotional and physical state and really ask yourself:

1. Where do I want to go? *toward enlightenment* *a blissful*
2. Who do I want to become? *and peaceful existance*
3. What is my life really about? *a caring, kind, compassionate at all times*
4. Who do I want to impact? *human being* *devoted to*
5. What do I want to create right now? *at the service of*
   peace now! others

Be outrageously playful, excited, and relentless. Trust that you know the answers—expect the answers and you will have them. If you need extra help, take out your *purple crayon* and take another stab at these questions.

family, friends, and people in need, want to help people

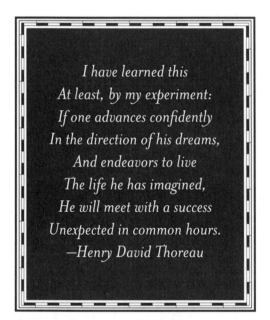

I have learned this
At least, by my experiment:
If one advances confidently
In the direction of his dreams,
And endeavors to live
The life he has imagined,
He will meet with a success
Unexpected in common hours.
—Henry David Thoreau

Building a Dynasty in a Day

It all started when my daughters were young, and I took them to amusement parks on Sunday. I sat on a bench eating peanuts and looking all around me. I said to myself, dammit, why can't there be a better place to take your children, where you can have fun together?
—Walt Disney

You've heard the saying, "Rome wasn't built in a day," used to illustrate that things take time. Although there is a fundamental truth to this statement, it is fundamentally flawed. Rome was built in a day, the way Disney World was built in a day. When good old Walt decided he was going to create a place for parents to take children and have fun together, Disney World was born. Naturally, it took more than a day to build the "greatest theme park on earth" physically, but the most critical component of the creation process was complete.

The creation process always begins with a thought. That's all it takes, one thought which you may have had in the last sixty seconds, or you may need to go through a few dozen, a few hundred, or a few thousand constructive thoughts before you find the one that will catalyze the birth of an empire.

Once you understand the power of a thought, you'll be well on your way to creating your *dynasty*. Humanity's most prolific thinkers have all illustrated the truth of this idea. English essayist James Allen wrote, "Man is the master of thought, the molder of character, and the maker and shaper of condition, environment, and destiny." Napoleon Hill, the author of the classic *Think and Grow Rich* discovered that, "Truly, 'thoughts are things,' and powerful things at that, when they are mixed with definiteness of purpose, persistence, and a burning desire for their translation into riches, or other material objects."

Now, it's your turn. It's time to begin building your own *dynasty*—one that brings you greater fulfillment while simultaneously providing immense value to the world around you. What idea do you have that can change the world? (Or perhaps just change you?)

> *Our life is what our thoughts make it.*
> *—Marcus Aurelius*

Momentum Manifesto

When you enter a state of tremendous momentum, you will be amazed at what happens. The dreams and desires you once thought were unattainable are now achieved effortlessly.

According to *Webster's Unabridged Dictionary*: Momentum, (1) the impetus of a moving object; (2) in mechanics, the quantity of motion of a moving object, equal to the product of its mass and its velocity. Neither are very helpful meanings for this discussion.

Momentum is the result of energy being focused in a particular area to gain a desired outcome. Momentum is something you have the power to create consciously whenever you desire, assuming you understand the steps and strategies for getting what you want.

The fastest way to create a momentum plan is to follow these three simple steps:

1. Clarify what you are building momentum toward—what do you want?
2. Ask yourself, "What has to happen to get this result?"
3. Brainstorm all the necessary actions you must take in the next 90 days to achieve the result.

When you follow these three simple steps, you will have a roadmap directing you to where you want to go. After you design your momentum plan, it is time to take action, capitalizing on the roadmap you have developed.

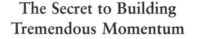

The Secret to Building Tremendous Momentum

To build tremendous momentum, design a concise, short-term strategic plan of essential actions necessary to achieve whatever results or goals you want.

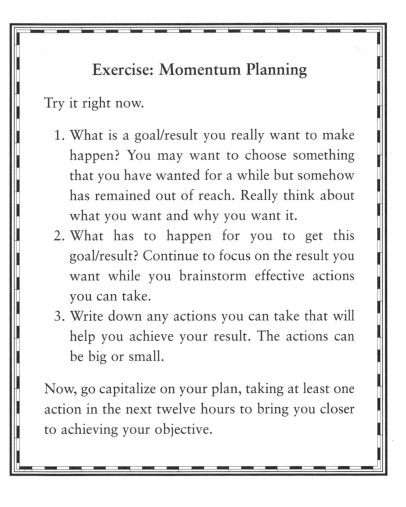

Exercise: Momentum Planning

Try it right now.

1. What is a goal/result you really want to make happen? You may want to choose something that you have wanted for a while but somehow has remained out of reach. Really think about what you want and why you want it.
2. What has to happen for you to get this goal/result? Continue to focus on the result you want while you brainstorm effective actions you can take.
3. Write down any actions you can take that will help you achieve your result. The actions can be big or small.

Now, go capitalize on your plan, taking at least one action in the next twelve hours to bring you closer to achieving your objective.

What Do You Want?

You will become as great as your dominant aspiration...
If you cherish a vision, a lofty ideal in your heart,
you will realize it.
—James Allen

What do you want? Such a simple question, isn't it? Yet, crazy as it seems, most people never take the time to honestly ask this question in order to figure out specifically what they want in their lives. People say things like, "I want a new job," or "I want to meet someone," or "I want more money." But they rarely get more specific. This lack of clarity will usually lead to continued lack of fulfillment. Those on the ***Journey*** have another way of approaching change.

You will never hear an ***Impossibility Seeker*** talking about what is not *perfect* in his life. He will never go to a friend or colleague and rant about credit card debt or a lack of physical energy. And why is that? He simply does not have time. He is too occupied determining exactly what results he wants and designing strategies for getting them. You must become a critical thinker, an expert at creating change and adding immense value to others' lives as well as your own.

So, what do *you* want? In your health? In your relationships? In your business or work? In your finances? Learning to consciously ask these questions and expect clear answers will lead you to a life of incredible fulfillment.

Make at least one decision about something you want to change in your life right now—something that will give you a satisfying sense of fulfillment. After you experience it once, you will be addicted to the feeling, and you will continue the process of all *Impossibility Seekers*, constantly making new distinctions and life-changing decisions by asking yourself, *"What do I want?"*

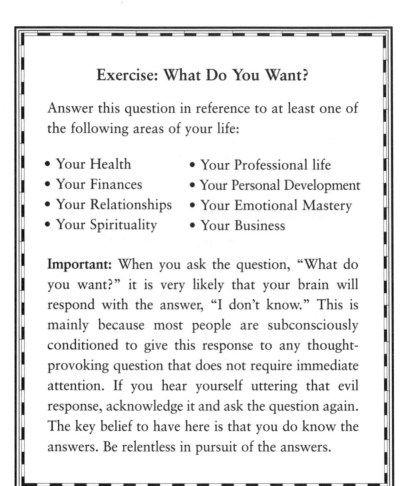

Exercise: What Do You Want?

Answer this question in reference to at least one of the following areas of your life:

- Your Health
- Your Finances
- Your Relationships
- Your Spirituality

- Your Professional life
- Your Personal Development
- Your Emotional Mastery
- Your Business

Important: When you ask the question, "What do you want?" it is very likely that your brain will respond with the answer, "I don't know." This is mainly because most people are subconsciously conditioned to give this response to any thought-provoking question that does not require immediate attention. If you hear yourself uttering that evil response, acknowledge it and ask the question again. The key belief to have here is that you do know the answers. Be relentless in pursuit of the answers.

White Marker, Blue Marker

If you don't know where you're going,
you'll end up someplace else.
—Yogi Berra

Fahnestock State Park is about an hour north of New York City, off the Taconic Parkway. This fantastic eleven-thousand-acre park is covered with sixty miles of terrific trails, diverse terrain, and all of nature's wonders. Being an avid hiker, I frequented this particular state park almost weekly for an entire autumn season.

After exploring the majority of the trails I fell into a pattern of going on one particular route that led to an incredibly isolated and scenic spot. At my private retreat, a big boulder overlooks a beautiful, small lake hidden in the woods. The ambience is quiet and peaceful—a great place to read, write, sleep, meditate, do Tai Chi or Yoga or whatever else you can imagine. I feel centered and relaxed just thinking about the spot.

Getting there was pretty straight forward and half the fun. I took the "White" trail (which was the Appalachian Trail) to the "Blue" trail and just followed it up and across a diverse range of terrain until I got to my magical spot.

One morning I was walking along the Appalachian Trail, on route to my spot when I heard some voices—and more intrusive—shouting, up ahead. As I got closer I saw it was a family with three kids. I struggled to hear what they were shouting. The leader of the group, the mother, was yelling something, and one by one each member shouted the same phrase.

I began to overtake the family on the narrow trail, smiling and saying hello to each person as I advanced. When I reached the front of the group, the leader turned and said with a smile, "It looks like we're going to have a new leader, guys." Returning the smile, I said, "I see. And what exactly does that mean and what are you shouting?" "The trail," she said with a big smile, "is marked by these white flares on the trees and since it's our first time out here, we want to make sure we don't get lost. So the leader yells 'white marker' when a new marker appears and each person repeats it so everyone hears."

"I see," I replied, "good thinking," winking playfully at the mother.

So playing along, I took the lead and began shouting "white marker" each time I passed one of the markers, getting a giggle from the kids on every shout. Walking at a significantly faster pace than the group, I quickly pulled out of range.

I readjusted to the quiet, serene beauty all around me, still chuckling every time I noticed a white marker. I walked for a while, until I noticed that the forest felt unfamiliar. Could I have missed my trail? Nah, I'd done this walk dozens of times. I could find the Blue trail blindfolded.

I continued onward still confused as to where my turn-off was. I came upon a group of backpackers and asked if they knew the whereabouts of the Blue trail. One of them pulled out a map (what a novel idea) and told me that I was about a mile and half away from the Blue trail; pointing in the direction I had just come. I thanked my fellow travelers and headed back, feeling confused and a little frustrated.

How did I miss the Blue trail? Then it hit me. Even though I wanted to take the Blue trail, I had been focusing on the white markers because of the family's game. I laughed at how crazy it was that I overshot my trail by a mile and a half—all because I did not focus on what I wanted.

Never discount the power of your thoughts toward directing the quality of your life—for the extraordinary or the miserable. *You move in the direction of your dominant thoughts—best you decide what those thoughts will be.*

The Three Laws of Creation

I will not reason and compare, my business is to create.
—William Blake

There are three fundamental *Laws of Creation* for getting what you want in your life:

First, you must **know you can** create anything. Notice that I didn't say "think" or "believe;" you have to **know** within yourself that you will find a way. We all possess the ability to create what we want; it's as innate to ourselves as our ability to breathe. The only difference is that some people have not had much practice up until now, because **creating** has **not** been a critical part of their life. You must cultivate this knowing in every thing you do. This doesn't mean you are not going to screw up from time to time, or all the time for that matter; it just means you will figure out a way.

Second, you must *decide what you want.* I know it sounds so simplistic but so many people leave this step out. Be specific. Saying, "I want more money," just won't cut it. How much more? A dollar? You have to be crystal clear about what you want if you truly want to create it. The greater your clarity, the more feasible the *creation.*

Third, like Harold, you must pick up your *purple crayon* and *draw like crazy.* This is the powerful principle of consistent action, where you stop talking about what you want and go make it happen. You understand that the *Journey* will not be easy—that you need to change your approach when you're not getting what you want. With *crayon* in hand, you cultivate the courage to go up against insurmountable odds. In the end, through consistent and intelligent action, you will be victorious.

The Wisdom to Know

Resolve to perform what you ought.
Perform without fail what you resolve.
—Benjamin Franklin

What does it mean to **know** you can create anything? Not *think*, not *believe*, but internally **know** you will find a way, no matter what, to turn your dreams into a physical reality?

When you **know** you have the power to create, it is no longer a question of "if," only a matter of "when." Your body's physiology and your thought patterns work in harmony, in a state of absolute resourcefulness, to come up with answers you just could not even imagine…yet. This amazing synergy of body and mind allows you to continually grow and discover an entirely new realm of being where you are in charge, defining your own rules.

Your state of *knowing* keeps you on track regardless of your environmental circumstances. Obstacles appear out of nowhere, barriers arise without warning, and your whole world turns upside down, but your *knowing* keeps you on your desired path.

Like in *Harold and the Purple Crayon*, your willingness to draw, to lift up that *crayon*, even when it seems immovable, is a fundamental necessity for the *Journey*. It takes a state of *knowing* to take continual hits but to keep going. It takes certainty and strength to press on despite major and minor setbacks, physical and emotional pain, and negative influences of others—to know you will create the unthinkable.

They can because they think they can.
—Virgil

The Director's Chair

Nurture your minds with great thoughts,
to believe in the heroic makes heroes.
—Benjamin Disraeli

It was a sunny and relatively warm Saturday for a Manhattan February afternoon. I was walking around Union Square enjoying the sun and watching the diverse crowd of people strolling and conversing on the surrounding park benches when a harsh winter breeze blew through the park. It was the kind of wind that just pierces down to the bone. I took shelter in one of my favorite entertainment zones in New York—the Virgin Megastore on 14th Street.

The store has two enormous floors that take up about half of the block. The main floor is all music, but following my usual routine, I headed down the escalator where all the movies, books, and magazines are located. In addition to the endless videos, DVDs, computer games, books, and magazines for sale, the floor has awesome movie kiosks— individual television screens with headsets, each playing different movies. The movies run for twenty minutes before resetting to the beginning.

I picked up the headset to the director's cut of *X-Men*, a movie I had already seen and really enjoyed. Just as I became completely enthralled by the picture, it stopped and started from the beginning. A little frustrated, I began casually walking the endless aisles picking up different items at random, simultaneously listening to a techno-esque tune being pumped through the store.

My imaginative thoughts took over my consciousness as I entered the realm of the *mutants*. I began theorizing the existence of mutants and questioning my own mutant abilities. (So where is Doctor Xavier, the leader and guardian of the *X-Men*, when you need him?)

I caught myself in this fantastic line of questioning and walked back to where the *X-Men* movie was playing. As I watched another moviegoer enthralled by the film I began to wonder…how could we use the power of movies to help create an extraordinary life? And what if there were a practical way to incorporate the *movie world* into our *real* life? Then it hit me.

Our lives are living, breathing movies! Our reality—how we experience the world—is nothing more than a great big movie, the quality of which is up to our own perceptual patterns. Our experiences and emotions create how we perceive the world, through our own human filters. The best part about this is that we are in the ***director's chair***!

You are in control of the movie and how things turn out. Now, obviously you can't control all the external events that take place in your life, but you can control how you react to a specific event and what that event will mean.

As a *director*, you can create an incredible love story, a romance to be remembered. You can create an unforgettable, action-packed adventure or a hilarious comedy. There are truly no boundaries to designing the movie that is your life. Your movie, that is, your life experience, is constrained only by a lack of imagination and a lack of passion for living.

The challenge comes when you are not consciously sitting in your ***director's chair***, and you let your movie become a compilation of external events without any meaning or purpose. When you are unconscious of your *film*, you tend to create ongoing dramas, heart-breaking after-school specials, and terrifying horror movies. But the choice is yours!

If you haven't already done so, begin right now to create a magical story that will withstand the test of time and have you living an extraordinary life.

So, what are the components of your movie that you need to be aware of? How do you design a magnificent story?

The Leading Role

The most important aspect of your magnificent story is YOU! This is *your* story and you better be the leading role. Every story needs a dynamic hero—the lead role that defines the quality and impact of the story. The hero is essential in mythical stories, modern-day movies, and certainly in everyday life. Why do you think big-name stars like Tom Hanks, Arnold Schwarzenegger, or Julia Roberts command around twenty million dollars per movie? We watch a film on the big screen and a part of us identifies with the lead character—the more potent the connection, the more successful the movie. James Bond and Indiana Jones films are perfect examples. We want, in many ways to be like these iconic heroes.

The process of defining the leading role is the process of creating your own identity—who you are and what you are about. The identity you create for yourself will help determine the decisions you make in the future and your overall quality of life.

Defining You

1. Who are you right now, mentally, physically, spiritually, financially, and socially?
2. Who do you want to become in the future? When you see yourself ten years from now, what's different? How have you grown? What can you now do with ease that once was just a far-reaching dream?

When answering the above questions, it is important to step into the person you want to become. Essentially, you must expand your identity and act as if you are the person you want to become. By doing so, your new beliefs about who you are and what you are capable of spawn entirely new and exciting life adventures.

Setting the Stage

Once you are clear about who you are, it is time to begin telling your magnificent story. Here too, you are setting yourself up to win by defining what you want to take place in the near future. This is an incredibly fun and powerful exercise that can shape the quality of your adventure. Setting the stage is similar to writing a screenplay. You are going to tell your story from start to finish—where does the story begin and how does it turn out? This is *your story*—the levels of excitement, fun, love, adventure, passion, and so on are all in the hands of the director (or playwright).

What is your story?

1. Where does the story begin?
2. Where will your story take you next?
3. Where will the story go from there?
4. What is the legacy you're going to leave behind?
5. What will the history books say about your adventure?

Cast of Characters

Next, cue the cast. Empowering supporting roles lift the lead role to new heights while unsupportive characters can literally destroy your life. Who is your supporting cast right now? Do they help you to become more, challenging you, growing with you, sharing both good and bad times? Or were you unconscious with the selection of your current *cast of characters*? If you were, I'd bet there's a bunch of "friends" that are actually keeping you from creating the life you deserve. These misguided cast members are not hindering your pursuit intentionally or vindictively, but the end result is you playing at a lower standard, feeling unfulfilled.

You can dream, create, design, and build the most beautiful place in the world, but it requires people to make it reality.
—Walt Disney

Everybody Needs a Theme Song

Every movie has a soundtrack. I always love a good movie soundtrack because it is like a recorded mix tape (or burned CD) with great songs from different bands. Great movies often have great soundtracks where just listening to a particular song can mentally take you back to that particular part in the movie. Why not create a soundtrack for your life—a roster of songs, each evoking particular emotions you want to experience. To go one step further, adopt a hilarious idea from the show, *Ally Mcbeal*. Ally (Calista Flockhart) and her colleague, John Cage (Peter Macnicol) both have theme songs they walk to and their songs can pop into their heads at random times. (Naturally the audience can hear the songs too—Ally's is *Tell Me* by The Exciters and John's is a Barry White track.) I love this idea. Find a moving, powerful song to become a part of who you are—just thinking about this song should bring you up to a higher level.

Exercise: Creating the Lead Role

After my revelation from watching *X-Men*, I had this immediate impulse to create a fun and powerful identity for myself so I could write an even more magical story and truly ***create the impossible*** in my own life. I went around the corner to a local coffee shop, sat down with my journal and began to write. I had no rules for the exercise, and I was in a playful mood.

I created a fantastic character that got me juiced. I thought of any descriptive, emotionally moving titles and character types I wanted to incorporate into my hero-identity, only writing down the ones that excited me. I went home, typed what I had into a one-page "bio" of my leading role. The character was mysterious and powerful, including many elements that I pulled from different fictional characters as well as traits that were already part of my identity. I didn't take myself too seriously, there was no judgment, and I was proud of what I had created.

In the days that followed, I noticed how an image of this character would pop into my head at random times. Subconsciously I had always been doing this, but now that I was consciously aware, I was able to tap into multiple aspects of my hero-self. The results were incredible! I was able to solve problems faster, communicate more effectively, and generally feel great on a more consistent basis. Plus, I was behaving in a more playful and passionate manner.

Before you create your new hero-identity, you can read mine called *The Alchemic Warrior*, as an example.

The Alchemic Warrior

Who is that man who walks quietly on that mysterious dark night—there one minute, gone the next? His long, brown suede cloak hangs loosely and sways calmingly in the midnight breeze. Under the cloak lies a man of incredible power, with a toned, strong muscular physique and a vibrant, youthful energy, which creates a luminous glow around his entire body. He is a man called by so many names, seen by many, understood by few. His true strength permeates from his heart, the purest of hearts, filled with so much unconditional love that he has no choice but to devote his life to the service of helping others.

Make no mistake, this extraordinary being is a warrior and a fighter. He has diligently studied the ways of both the ninja and the samurai while training in eleven different forms of martial arts and weaponry. He is well versed in the art of war and combat, being a master strategist and a wise tactician. His unmatched abilities to think creatively and positively influence others have made him a visionary leader.

But in his heart, this warrior still walks alone. For he is a traveler. His quest to serve has molded him into an explorer and adventurer and taken him to far and distant exotic lands and to the heart of hundreds of cities. Like any true traveler, he demonstrates a chameleon-like ability to adapt to any situation. His wandering nature has helped him combine his warrior mentality with that of a poet and a philosopher.

And so it is true: One cannot be a great warrior without being a great healer, for it is not wars that make one great but the ability for the good in you to conquer evil. This great man is the healer of healers—a man who constantly practices his art while continuing to explore old and new ways of healing both individuals and the planet.

To be continued...

Now, it's your turn. Remember, the only rule is to be playful—have fun with this, there are no right or wrong answers—just trust yourself and go! Grab a pen and paper, a bound journal (if you have one), and create your new lead role.

So, who are you now? Do you love your new hero-self? Is this leading role going to win multiple Oscar's for your award-deserving (winning) performance? Read it over a few times later today and see how it feels. Get rid of what doesn't excite you and feel free to add whatever additional components you want.

Five Magic Words

I will live this day as if it is my last.
—Og Mandino

This may be your last day, and in the end, it's not how long you live, it's how you live. If you don't take the time to give thanks and acknowledge how incredible it is just simply to be alive, you miss out on the juice of life because you are unconscious of all the beauties and wonders of each moment.

Regardless of how great or troublesome your life may appear right now, it is a miracle that you are alive—that you are breathing; that you have the gift of sight; that you have the ability to read and comprehend; that you are above ground. At any moment, there are an infinite number of things you can be thankful for. Life truly is a gift that most of us do not appreciate—we look for *more* without ever acknowledging how lucky we are right now!

This simple practice will transform your life forever. It is so simple that many people will discount its immeasurable value, missing the power of this little practice.

> Each morning as soon as you awake, smile and give thanks for the awesome power of today by saying these *five magic words*:
>
> ***"Thank you for this day."***

This small act of gratitude will produce amazing results in every area of your daily life. ***Thank you for this day.*** Five incredibly powerful words. These words can be a prayer or just an incantation that you say (whatever is best for you).

Why is this phrase so powerful? What are the first things people usually say or think when they wake up in the morning? For many, it's phrases like:

> *"Oh man, not another day at work."*
> *"I wish I could sleep longer."*
> *"I'm so tired."*
> *"I don't want to get up."*

Wouldn't you rather wake up each morning and induce feelings of gratitude and excitement instead of feelings of lethargy and depression? Your life is a gift and the more you treasure it on a moment-to-moment basis, the greater life experience you will have.

What can you be thankful for right now?

- Your breath
- Your body
- Your heart
- The sun
- Your smile
- Trees & forests

- Your family
- Your friends
- Your mind
- Your ability to love
- Your ability to learn
- Seasons & nature

What else can you be thankful for right now? In any instance, we have a great deal to be thankful for. Without a strong sense of gratitude, we'll never fully experience true bliss in life.

Also, every night before drifting to sleep, take a deep breath. Inhale all the joys of the day and give thanks once more, for today may be your last. And if you wake the next morning, rejoice and make this day even more awesome than the last. Begin each day and end each night with this new ritual.

Try it right now. Put down this book and close your eyes.
Take a deep breath, make a big smile and say,
"Thank you for this day."

When each day is the same as the next,
it's because people fail to recognize
the good things that happen in their lives
every day that the sun rises.
—Paulo Coelho

Ten Questions for Creating a Glorious Day

Happy the man, and happy he alone,
He, who can today his own:
He who, secure within, can say:
"To-morrow, do thy worst, for I have liv'd to-day."
—Horace

What if there were ***ten questions*** that could help you create the greatest day in your entire life? Would you be willing to ask each question with the resolve to find an answer? Would this be a valuable practice to incorporate into your daily routine? Would this be worth your precious time?

Do this for ten days: Within an hour of waking up, review each question on the next page and put your energy into coming up with quality answers. Then go do it!

Stay conscious of any big and small changes that take place in your life.

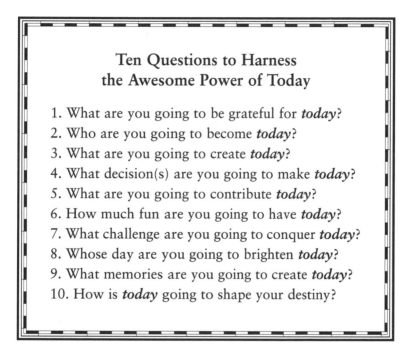

Ten Questions to Harness
the Awesome Power of Today

1. What are you going to be grateful for *today*?
2. Who are you going to become *today*?
3. What are you going to create *today*?
4. What decision(s) are you going to make *today*?
5. What are you going to contribute *today*?
6. How much fun are you going to have *today*?
7. What challenge are you going to conquer *today*?
8. Whose day are you going to brighten *today*?
9. What memories are you going to create *today*?
10. How is *today* going to shape your destiny?

Follow Your Fire

Follow your bliss.
—Joseph Campbell

"Fire is one of the human race's essential tools, control of which helped start it on the path toward civilization," as explained by the *Encyclopedia Britannica*. Now, you must harness the power of a different fire, a fire that burns within you. In order to create what you want in your life, you must learn to ***follow your fire***. You have a flame burning within you, which when tapped, provides an infinite reservoir of energy, power, and possibility. Think of it like a pilot light in an oven that never goes out, always there. Your fire is an eternally burning source of passion, enthusiasm, and excitement.

You may be someone that's constantly tapping into your *fire*, always energized and ready to go. You find yourself getting up early and staying up late. You never feel like you're working. When you talk about what you're doing with your life, a big smile surfaces and your whole face glows. You're constantly generating feelings of love, excitement, and joy. You never find it necessary to judge yourself or others because you're too busy finding ways to add value, serve others and create what you want. You get excited just thinking about what you do every day!

This is the incredible drive that all those on the *Journey* learn to access on a consistent basis. Once you do, there is no barrier or blockade that someone can put in your path that will keep you from getting where you want to go.

Do you know who are the best at tapping into their *fire* consistently? Kids are awesome at living unbridled passion, aren't they? They wake up in the morning ready to go with positive anticipation, playing and celebrating life. Whenever I sleep over at my aunt's and uncle's house during the holidays, I never need an alarm clock because at around 6:30 A.M. I get at least two kids jumping on top of me, excited to start the day. That's what we all need to tap into—we must become a playful, passionate soul living on purpose.

Everything comes if a man will only wait. I have brought myself by long meditation to the conviction that a human being with a settled purpose must accomplish it, and that nothing can resist a will that will stake even existence for its fulfillment.
—Benjamin Disraeli

For Those Who Feel Their Fire Burned Out...

Fear not! The flame never dies. It's still within you right now, waiting in child-like anticipation to be rekindled. Ask yourself these two questions with positive anticipation of finding the answers:

1. *If I knew I couldn't fail, what would I do with my life right now?*
2. *If money were not an issue, what would I do for a living (professionally)?*

Tap into your fire right now by doing what you love to do—and invigorate your soul.

Stop and Look Around

Life moves pretty fast. If you don't stop and look around
for a while, you could miss it.
—Ferris Bueller

On your quest to the *impossible*, you may adopt a go-go-go mentality, without stopping for a moment to appreciate what you already have. When was the last time you randomly stopped what you were doing, took a deep breath, smiled and thought about the precious gift of each moment? Matter of fact, when was the last time you smiled for no good reason? Try it right now...*smile* and *laugh*! Come on, no one's watching. Put a big, silly grin on your face and laugh out loud. Think about how lucky you are to be alive. Notice how you feel. If you are really smiling, you feel a great sensation moving through your body, and you're saying to yourself, "Hmmm, I should do this more often." Well, don't let me stop you, go right ahead, smile, laugh and feel lucky for no reason on a regular basis.

Have you ever passed someone who was smiling or laughing and then found yourself smiling? Sometimes we're unconscious of this viral reaction. The smile opens doorways to a whole new universe. You'll find it easier to meet people, and more specifically, you'll find more people interested in talking to you. If you look at a person when his face is tense, frowning, and distraught compared to when he is smiling and happy, he looks like two different people. A frowning person usually looks downright unattractive, while a simple smile causes a beautiful transformation. Try it for yourself: Go to a mirror and put an intense frown on your face and then a big smile. Notice the difference.

With today's fast-moving lifestyle and rapid technological advances, there's more and more stuff to be busy with. Whether it's a cell phone, a PDA (personal digital assistant like a Palm Pilot®, for you non-techies), email, pagers, or one of the hundreds of new gadgets that is always in development, we are constantly in demand from our environment. We can either say, "Well, I might as well just accept this as the way things are—there's nothing I can do about it." Or, you can take charge of your life.

How? *Simply stop and look around.* These are immortal words spoken by that tenacious high school student who understood the principles of living in the moment and seizing the day. You must develop the skill of bringing yourself back to the present when the moment seems to slip away. Life can be so much fun if we only learn to actually *live each moment*.

Give the Gift of a Smile

Why should you give someone, including yourself, the gift of a smile?

1. Smiles are contagious—you'll cause others to smile too.
2. Smiling makes you look more attractive—it's easier to meet people.
3. Smiling helps promote a healthier body and a directed mind.
4. Smiling will make you feel happier and more alive.

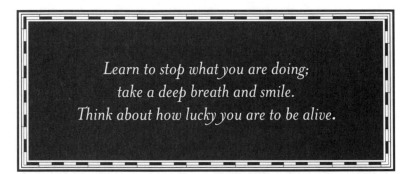

Learn to stop what you are doing;
take a deep breath and smile.
Think about how lucky you are to be alive.

Never Look Back

Life is full of amazing phenomena.

Each day we learn more and more.

With this constant accumulation of knowledge we are
able to enjoy each day with greater success than the last.

But, we can't look back.

When we look back, we lose this irreplaceable, special moment.

And why should we?

If we believe that every moment is more glorious than the next,
A moment filled with infinite possibilities,
Why would we look back and miss out on all the beauty
and magic that exist in the present?

–Scott Jeffrey

The String Quartet

I lived in London for a short time. I have tons of wonderful memories, many of which came from my favorite secret spot. I'm going to share it with you, but you have to promise that you won't tell anyone else about it. It'll be our little secret.

At the south end of Covent Gardens there is a large building with different craft shops and eateries, called Covent Gardens Market. The neighboring streets are cobblestone and for pedestrians only (no cars allowed). On any given day, street performers ranging from new-age musicians to advanced juggling and magic acts decorate the streets, commanding crowds of tourists and locals alike. Downstairs at the far end of the market is an old, cavernous restaurant with additional outside seating in what looks like a sunken courtyard. You can sit, relax, sip some coffee or wine and watch people for hours. Others bring friends to engage in stimulating conversations about life and current events. I usually went alone.

At the far corner of the courtyard, underneath the stairs, there are different teams of string quartets that rotate in and out all day to perform for the crowd. Each quartet has its own personality and set of classical music they usually play. They appear to be your quintessential "starving" but talented artists and the whole experience was free. (I always threw at least a pound or two into their tip basket, but I knew I was getting the better end of the deal.)

There is something unusually captivating about this place. There I was, in the middle of an enormous metropolitan city with over seven million people, yet my surroundings were a safe haven of peace and tranquility. I would go at least once or twice a week and stay for hours. I brought books to read but I spent most of my time people-watching and getting lost in the beauty of live classical music. A quartet would play Pachelbel's Canon in D major, and a crowd would form around the upstairs railing. The people at the tables would chat away, sipping wine and munching on freshly sliced cheese and fruit. I would sit and consciously breathe, putting my life on hold for a few hours and completely immersing myself in the environment—it was surreal. I was able to let go and truly be in that moment.

Whenever I recall those times, a big smile comes to my face. Now would be one of those times.

We all have our own *String Quartets*—those magic moments in our lives. By simply recalling the experiences and telling the stories, we can relive these magic moments as often as we choose. Give yourself that gift.

Remember to Play

Those who bring sunshine to the lives of others
cannot keep it from themselves.
—Sir James Barrie

In our pursuit to design the unthinkable and live the
impossible life, we tend to get fairly intense along the way.
For good reasons too: We have loads of people all around us
giving us reasons why it won't work. We have a multitude
of references showing that success is highly improbable, and
yet here we are moving full speed ahead to create our
dreams. Who wouldn't be intense?

The challenge is that intensity without balance can lead
to anxiety, worry, stress, frustration, and anger (to name a
few negative side effects). Does this mean you can't get
intense in pursuing your life aspirations? Of course not.
Just be cognizant and do not lose sight of what's most

important to you. Each of us has different values and priorities in our lives and it is up to us to make sure we stay aligned with those values. Gravity pulls us toward getting caught up in the exciting roller coaster of life, filled with sharp turns, unexpected loops, and bone-crunching nose dives. The excitement and fear often take our focus away from what's important and what matters most in our lives. We get caught up in the day-to-day stuff and live in the pressures and demands of the moment.

As often as possible, take a step back for a moment, take a long, deep breath and remind yourself why you are doing all of this in the first place. Reconnect with the fun, playful side of you—the side that loves playing full out like a little kid. A little kid doesn't get intense and stressed out about his life (except when they are tired or hungry). Instead, kids smile, laugh and have loads of fun. What if you could act like a kid again and play while you actively pursued your deepest desires? What if that was *possible*?

Run with Your Hair on Fire

The *Journey to the Impossible* requires you to play like a kid. More. More. More. Always wanting to play more. Until someone says it's time to go to sleep. Then you continue to play in the dark for hours on end. You've gotta **run with your hair on fire**, like there is no tomorrow.

I remember when I was a kid. I always hated going to sleep. The thought of ending my day was always a painful process—for my mom as well. She spent hours each night trying to get me to go to sleep, usually to no avail. After being read several books, I would listen to a record of some musical. Unfortunately for my mom, auto-repeat cassette players hadn't hit the market yet so I would howl for her to turn the album over—again and again and again. I loved each day too much to throw in the towel.

We must develop and harness that same thrill, passion, and excitement for life! Then, achieving **impossible results** becomes a part of you. We create for the fun of it with incredible intensity—always moving forward, conceiving more, designing more, building more, and loving every minute of it. Most people like to stop. They come home from jobs that hold little meaning for them. They can't wait to grab quick dinners and plop in front of their TVs. These people rarely have much fun, rarely break the rules, and consequently, rarely create anything of lasting value.

Just to clarify—I'm not saying it's wrong to kick back and relax once in a while. I'm saying you don't want to live in that state. That is, not if you want to *master impossible living*.

You've got to love what you do and live with a seemingly unnatural exuberance for life. Because you love what you do and truly embrace each day, you don't feel constricted by the limiting boundaries other people live by or the rules that other people follow. Life isn't so black and white to you. You continue to try new things in a feverish pace for the fun of new experiences and new creations.

A Real Life Creator

Never tell a young person that anything cannot be done.
God may have been waiting centuries for someone ignorant
enough of the impossible to do that very thing.
—John Andrew Holmes

Imagine being fifteen-years-old, a popular kid, and a great student. Imagine being an active athlete with a passion for skiing. Imagine waking up on an otherwise average morning without any feeling in your legs, unable to simply turn yourself over in bed. Imagine how your life would be forever altered if one day a freak condition took hold of your body, committing you to a wheelchair for the rest of your life. How would you react? How would your life change? What would you think? What would you do?

As a freshman in high school, my cousin Eric Katz was

diagnosed with Transverse Myelitys, a condition where the immune system attacks the spinal cord. Eric went into a rehabilitation center where he was told he had about a fifty percent chance of regaining muscles in his legs, but Eric remained positive about being on his feet again soon. With Transverse Myelitys, if you do not walk within the first three months, the chances of ever walking again are minimal. Eric quickly passed the three-month mark, still in a wheelchair.

I could tell you a story about Eric's adjustment to a physically challenged life, about all the changes he had to make, and all the things he was no longer able to do. However, Eric never really focused on that stuff, so why should I? While many people in his situation might feel sorry for themselves, feeling intense feelings of anger, hurt, and depression, Eric simply did not have time.

Eric was too busy discovering a whole new world he is now a part of—a world with no boundaries or limitations, where his wheelchair became an asset instead of a liability. Eric began with track, an area he never had much interest in as an able-body. His first time on the track, he could not keep pace with a kid half his age; his arms gave out from sheer exhaustion. Eric was now committed to becoming a star athlete, training hard each day, progressing at an exponential rate. Within a year he was competing on a national level, building incredible upper body strength and continually breaking national records in the junior division.

Has Eric's life changed? Sure. Now, he has the opportunity

to travel all around the world, competing, and being more active than ever before. He now has the opportunity to learn about himself and grow emotionally at an accelerated rate. He now has the opportunity to surround himself with an incredible group of people who support and empower him to become more. Now, Eric has friends in every state in the country through his national competitions.

Eric's life is certainly different, but not in the way most people would expect. His life was transformed from the experience.

Three years later, Eric still loves track and is more excited about playing basketball now than he ever was before the wheelchair. That's a good thing too, since he is on scholarship at the University of Arizona for his remarkable athleticism.

So what's next for this daring and courageous *Creator of the Impossible*? Well, the 2004 Paralympics in Greece, of course. Why the Paralympics? Eric says with conviction, "It's out there, and I have to get it. It's just another goal." Like all *Creators*, Eric wants to be the best in the world and he is constantly setting higher standards to get there. How many people could say they woke up at 5:30 A.M. for practice six days a week during college? In addition to a full course load, Eric continues his training after class each day.

Probably the most amazing thing about this teen is that he's awesome to be around. He's happy and positive, in tune with the world around him. He relishes in living the *impossible life*, embracing each moment, and loving everything he does. And as for skiing, well, let's just say he has discovered a new passion for Mono skiing, a special ski designed for the physically challenged. Nothing can stop this guy.

You can't always control the external events in your life, but you can always control your reaction to those events. What's keeping you from living the *impossible life*?

Thank you, Eric, for being you.

Salutation to the Dawn

Look to this day!
For it is life, the very life of life.
In its brief course,
Lie all the verities and realities of your existence:
    The bliss of growth
        The glory of action
            The splendor of beauty.
For yesterday is but a dream
And tomorrow is only a vision,
But today well lived makes every yesterday a dream of happiness
And every tomorrow a vision of hope.
Look well, therefore, to this day!
Such is the salutation of the dawn.

–Kalidasa

CULTIVATING
IMPOSSIBLE
CREATIVITY

The Nature of Genius

$$E = mc^2$$

"There is no use trying," said Alice; "one can't believe impossible things." "I dare say you haven't had much practice," said the Queen. "When I was your age, I always did it for half an hour a day. Why, sometimes I've believed as many as six impossible things before breakfast."
—*Lewis Carroll*

What do Albert Einstein, Leonardo da Vinci, Galileo Galilee, and Sir Isaac Newton all have in common? Yes, they're all dead, but besides that? They're each considered **geniuses**. What does that mean? What is a genius and how do you become one?

If you look up the word **genius** in either *Webster's Dictionary* or the *American Heritage Dictionary* you'll find something very interesting. Most people define **genius** by exceptional mental capacity and intellectual prowess, which are part of the dictionary definition. Before that, in both dictionaries, you'll see *extraordinary creative powers*. Here lies the magic behind *genius*.

The above-mentioned scientists or anyone else you deem a modern-day *genius* are so because they have learned an essential skill for doing the unthinkable. They've all learned how to tap into their innate creative powers and unlock their *genius*.

How can you and I tap into this force, causing a personal transformation of our own mental capacity and intellectual prowess? It's a brain drug...no it's a special herb...no wait, it's banging our head against the wall while reciting *Puff the Magic Dragon*. Actually, there's no magic secret or mystical force. The real solution is very simple and very effective.

A *genius* is someone who **thinks differently** than everyone else! Let's repeat that: *A genius is someone who thinks differently than everybody else!* Right? Doesn't that make sense? Look at Leonardo da Vinci, one of my favorite **Impossibility Seekers** who *Journeyed to the Impossible* in the arts, science, invention, human physiology, and botany. Leonardo was able to consistently produce awe-inspiring results in so many areas of life by questioning everything and always staying curious.

I have a question for you: Can you think differently than everybody else? You and I both know the answer is "yes," and that's a good thing because it's an essential ingredient for achieving *impossible results*.

The question isn't, "Can I be a genius?" It's, "How do

I think like a genius?" In fact, the word *genius* is often inappropriately used to describe someone. We all have "genius moments," where you come up with an unusually clever idea or solution to a problem or you say something that blows all your friends away at the dinner table. It's these moments that define what it is to be a *genius*, the only difference is that someone who is perceived to be a *genius* has those moments on a more consistent basis.

Conversely, just as one can have *genius moments*, one can also have *moron moments*. Unfortunately, we've all had those too, such as when you can't correctly count your change in a grocery store or you momentarily forget how to spell the word "how." The *genius* within seems to be out to lunch, and you're left with thoughts like, "Is I a college graduate?"

I am enough of an artist to draw freely upon my imagination.
Imagination is more important than knowledge.
Knowledge is limited. Imagination encircles the world.
—Albert Einstein

The Creative Creed

Anytime you need a bright idea or a fast solution and you feel like your creative juices are nearly drained, remind yourself of the Creative Creed:

There is an infinite reservoir of ideas within me.

I will ask empowering questions and I will be patient with the answers.

I will encourage the creative process and never judge or criticize my thinking.

I will play and have fun, being outrageous and adventurous in everything I do.

I will look for ways to add immense value to the world around me.

I have the power to create.

The Whiteboard Economy

To improve is to change; to be perfect is to change often.
—Winston Churchill

What is the one thing all startup businesses have in common? The **whiteboard** is the ultimate symbol of creativity and the quintessential drawing tablet for our *purple crayons*, or rather, purple markers. On these beautifully shiny white surfaces, ideas are born, and more efficient ways of doing things are discovered. It's brainstorming at its finest. A team of people can stand around with different experiences and ideas (and colored markers) with a common goal in mind and literally design a future, a product, or a service that can change the world.

I've seen companies with rooms literally filled with whiteboards covering every inch of the wall—a glorious sight indeed. There's a highly portable version of the white-board. The technical term, I believe is "napkin." How many brilliant business concepts have been conceived on those small, folded, coffee-stained pieces of paper?

We live in a time of unprecedented change where remarkable innovation is not something that happens every couple of years, but rather, as fast as every three months. Product life cycles have shrunk from every ten years, down to every quarter. Change in our economy is happening so quickly that we are becoming almost desensitized to it. A few years ago you thought people with cell phones were arrogant and egotistical. Now you get irritated when your phone loses service. And we're just getting started. Exciting technological advancements will continue, creating markets and industries that are either in their infancies or have not yet been established.

What does all this mean for you? It means you must constantly find new ways to innovate and grow in both your personal and professional life. It means committing to a life of constant growth and learning. It means you must constantly be pursuing new strategies and making new distinctions that will add to your quality of life. It means you must come from a highly resourceful state, from a place where you know you can create anything. You must know there is always more. You must know that resting on your laurels is one of the most destructive things you can do and a sure way of losing what you have. Brainstorming and idea generation are not restricted to business alone. ***Adopt the habit of brainstorming in every area of life***.

You must constantly be brainstorming ideas of what you want to create and how to go about creating it. In the process, you will be developing your "solution dexterity"— a skill enabling you to tackle any obstacle and anticipate future challenges. Remember, your *purple crayon* is your new tool. Like the carpenter's hammer, this tool will help you build a magical empire of lasting value bound by nothing but the limitations of your heart and imagination.

> *If you do what you've always done,*
> *you'll get what you've always gotten.*
> —*Anonymous*

The Magic of Mind Mapping

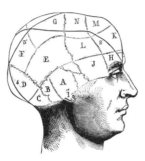

The best way to get a good idea is to get a lot of ideas.
—Linus Pauling

Mind mapping is a creative process, developed by Tony Buzan, the author of *The Mind Map Book: How to Use Radiant Thinking to Maximize Your Brain's Untapped Potential*. Mind mapping is the process of free-associating with pictures, words, and images. Mind mapping is an effective tool for linking the right (creative) and left (analytical) sides of your brain, helping to facilitate the creative process.

To begin the process, create a central image or word concept in the center of a blank sheet of paper (preferably unruled). Begin freely associating words and drawing images stemming from the central idea. You may find it helpful to write the purpose of your particular mind map in the top right corner of the page. Have fun with the exercise. Use different colors and make imaginative drawings—play like a kid and be outrageous. You'll be astonished when you see the results of your work, with new ideas springing from the page.

Mind mapping can be used for general brainstorming, solution-finding/problem solving, goal projecting, and more. Mind mapping can also be used when writing or reading a book. Mind mapping can be as simple or intricate as you desire.

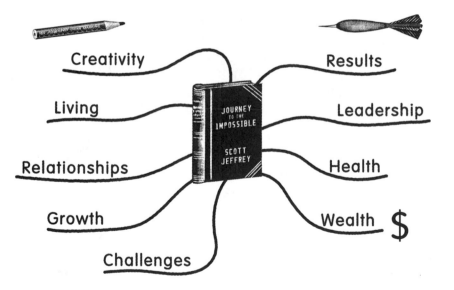

The Secret Behind Innovation

*The important thing is not to stop questioning. Curiosity has
its own reason for existing. One cannot help but be in awe
when he contemplates the mysteries of eternity, of life, of the
marvelous structure of reality. It is enough if one tries merely
to comprehend a little of this mystery every day.*
—Albert Einstein

Creativity. Imagination. Innovation. Hidden deep beneath
the mysterious caverns of the creative process lies an
enchanting secret—the *secret behind innovation*.

The secret is the magic of questions. To discover innovative ideas, you must ask innovative questions. To realize
imaginative solutions, ask imaginative questions. To be an
Impossible Innovator, ask questions that are different from
what everyone else is asking. Consciously or not, you are

constantly asking yourself questions, and it is the quality of these questions that defines your ability to think and act creatively. These questions ultimately define the quality of your life.

Questions like, "Why am I still in debt?" or "Why am I so fat?" are not going to propel you forward in life. While questions like, "How can I create more and add lasting value to people's lives?" or "How can I become unbelievably fit while gaining incredible energy and stamina in the process?" will help move you to where you want to go. The latter types of questions will stimulate your brain, getting you excited to come up with innovative answers.

This is an invaluable skill that you must master in order to consistently achieve *impossible results*. Remember, what you are striving to attain, others have tried and failed. To achieve *impossible results* you must think differently, not limiting your thought process to the same questions everyone else is asking.

There's a particular type of question that is ideal for *creating the impossible*—"What if?" questions. "What if?" questions bring you into a world of infinite possibilities. "What if?" questions lead you to other thought-provoking questions and more innovative solutions.

What if one question
could change your life forever?

In the imaginative phase, you ask questions such as: What if?
Why not? What rules can we break? What assumptions can
we drop? How about if we looked at this backwards? Can we
borrow a metaphor from another discipline? The motto of the
imaginative phase is: Thinking something different.
—Roger von Oech

The Art of Rule Breaking

*There are no limitations to the mind
except those we acknowledge.
—Napoleon Hill*

One of the critical rules for everyone, especially entrepreneurs, living in today's world—in fact, *the rule*—is that **there are no rules.** Remembering this will help you stay alert and more competitive in today's fast-moving way of life. You simply can't afford to let debilitating limitations or preconceived notions hinder your pursuit of the *impossible* in any area of your life.

So how do you cultivate the ***art of rule breaking***? First, I must make a small clarification. By *rule breaking*, I don't mean running a red light, cheating on a test or committing some other offensive violation of the law or your own moral and ethical standards. When I say *"rule breaking,"* I mean breaking through the usual, the norm, the expected, the status quo, "reality" as everyone else sees it. *Rule breaking* is about barreling through the norm like a guided torpedo—high velocity, high agility, and dead set on where it wants to go.

With the whirlwind of information and exciting stimuli of everyday activities, it's a challenge to consciously stay aware of the common limitations trap. Our brains use generalizations and rules to help evaluate situations and information that is critical when making a quick decision based on limited information. However, on our never-ending *Journey*, we must make *rule breaking* a habit, something we do consistently as a way of life.

Here's to the crazy ones, the misfits, the rebels, the trouble-makers, the round pegs in a square hole, the ones who see things differently. They're not fond of rules, and they have no respect for the status quo. You can quote them, disagree with them, glorify, or vilify them. About the only thing you can't do is ignore them, because they change things. They push the human race forward, and while some may see them as the crazy ones, we see genius, because the people who are crazy enough to think they can change the world are the ones who'll do it.
—Apple Computer Advertisement

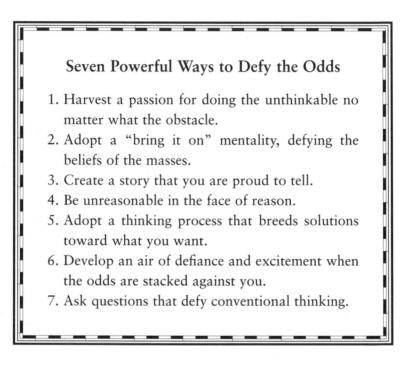

Seven Powerful Ways to Defy the Odds

1. Harvest a passion for doing the unthinkable no matter what the obstacle.
2. Adopt a "bring it on" mentality, defying the beliefs of the masses.
3. Create a story that you are proud to tell.
4. Be unreasonable in the face of reason.
5. Adopt a thinking process that breeds solutions toward what you want.
6. Develop an air of defiance and excitement when the odds are stacked against you.
7. Ask questions that defy conventional thinking.

The Power of Playful Defiance

You see things and say, "Why?"
But I dream things that never were, and I say, "Why not?"
—George Bernard Shaw

What if creating ***impossible results*** was a game? How much fun would you have creating the unimaginable? Could you do it? Is it *possible*?

You've heard of people like this all your life. They defy conventional thinking; they break all the rules, delivering an astounding end product. People like Bill Gates, Richard Branson, Oprah Winfrey, Albert Einstein, Michael Jordan, and Tiger Woods are just a few extraordinary individuals who have, in some way, mastered the ***Journey*** and defined a life on their own terms.

All of these people and anyone who creates anything of great value has adopted a vital attitude, one of ***playful defiance***—whether they're conscious of it or not. ***Playful*** *defiance* is a "bring it on" mentality. It's a developed air of defiance and excitement that causes you to take action whenever everyone says, "It can't be done." It's a psychology that breeds solutions and actions toward what you want, instead of what you don't want. It's a mentality you cultivate within yourself, a burning desire, a relentless determination when the odds are stacked against you.

You do it for the love of the game. You do it for the love of creating an amazing story. You do it for the love of conquering the unconquerable and turning everything upside down.

> *It's a funny thing about life; if you refuse to accept*
> *anything but the best, you very often get it.*
> *—W. Somerset Maugham*

An Impossible Example

I've always loved the play Peter Pan, and I've never wanted to grow up. I'm a bit of a maverick. I love people, I love challenge, I love taking on the establishment, I love turning things upside down and having fun while doing it. I love motivating people, I love to achieve the impossible. I don't want to waste a minute of my life.
—Richard Branson

One of the best examples of a rule breaker, and perhaps the iconic image of *playful defiance*, is Richard Branson. Richard, or I should say, Sir Richard, is the creator of the Virgin empire, consisting of the Virgin Megastores, Virgin Atlantic Airways, and more than 150 other companies within the Virgin fold. His estimated net worth hovers around three billion dollars, and the Virgin brand is ranked the third most recognized brand in England.

But this wildly successful British businessman is not your typical CEO type. He is often called the P.T. Barnum of British business because of his outrageous publicity stunts, like putting on a dress to help launch Virgin Brides or driving a World War II tank through Times Square and firing on Coca Cola to launch the challenge against Virgin Cola. When he's not creating another Virgin business, he's off on some adventure like attempting to be the first man to fly around the world in a hot-air balloon. To say this man is outrageous would be an understatement.

Let's take a look at some of the philosophies this extraordinary *Impossibility Seeker* lives by and applies to his businesses. An interviewer once asked Branson: "How do you keep reinventing yourself over and over? Don't you get tired?" Branson responded:

> *"Sometimes yes. I like to burn the candle at both ends. It's self-inflicted. I like to throw myself wholeheartedly into life. Now I find myself in this fantastic position—I could do almost anything I could possibly want to do, and I just don't want to waste that position by disappearing off to a desert island and putting my feet up. There is so much more to learn and to achieve, and so much more fun to have, and so I choose to continue to*

set myself new challenges, to set our staff new challenges, new goals to overcome. And as we get comfortable, I want to make sure that we shake ourselves up and don't let ourselves get too comfortable—that we keep questioning what we're doing, keep questioning what other people are doing, keep questioning what big companies are doing, seeing whether we can turn them on their heads, and pay the bills at the same time."

Richard Branson's Five Criteria for the Virgin Label:

1. It must have high quality.
2. It must be innovative.
3. It must provide good value for the money.
4. It must be challenging to existing alternatives.
5. It must have a sense of fun.

Branson takes on companies like British Airways and Coca Cola, and he often wins. This man thrives on creating and doing stuff that others say is *impossible*. And does he fail? You better believe it. But he has fun in the process, laughs at himself and moves on to his next challenge. Richard Branson has a craving for turning *impossibilities* into raging successes. His wild energy and showmanship have made him a celebrity, a figure who projects a larger-than-life image. People love Sir Richard because he fights for the good of the people, consistently adding value, but also because he makes things happen. He's a fantastic example that proves you can create whatever you want in your life.

Be Unreasonable

Be totally and undeniably unreasonable. Be unreasonable in your expectations for what you want in life. Be unreasonable about your demands of yourself and your standards emotionally, physically, socially, and financially. Be unreasonable in the level of joy and happiness that you experience on a moment-to-moment basis. Be unreasonable because it is your duty—you owe it to yourself. Anything less is settling for less than your best and will hinder your ability to achieve *impossible results*.

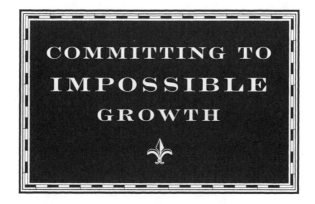

COMMITTING TO
IMPOSSIBLE
GROWTH

The Traveler's Way

Journal Entry Excerpt
2:18 P.M., June 29, 1997
Costa Rica

Adaptability. Travelers must possess this trait. We learn that our emotions do not have to be governed by externalities. We learn to accept both the good and the bad as experiences. We learn to embrace every moment because it is all we have. We take strength in knowing four enchanting words, "This too shall pass." We know the world is vast and magnificent, full of all of God's creations. We meet different people, different cultures, different religions, and different ways of thinking. We meet this great diversity with the knowledge that no one way is right or better than another—just different. We expand our minds, breaking any and all boundaries and limitations to which we once clung so closely. We travel different roads, learning and growing every day. Through our acceptance of what is, we cultivate the traveler's trait of adaptability—to any and all situations. For we know it is all but a new experience, yet another step on the path of the unknown.

Adaptability is the traveler's weapon. With it comes adventure, influence, and prosperity. Without it, the traveler shall certainly perish.

–Scott Jeffrey

The Human Sponge

*Never regard study as a duty, but as the enviable opportunity
to learn—to know the liberating influence of beauty in the
realm of the spirit—for your own personal joy and to the profit
of the community to which your later work belongs.*
—Albert Einstein

Everything must grow or die. This is a basic law of life.
The key to our evolution and fulfillment is our **growth**. The
more we grow, the more we become. We must constantly be
absorbing information and learning to continually grow
and expand. As a ***human sponge***, you can take in new
information at dizzying rates, use what you need and discard the rest. The cool thing about being a ***human sponge***
is that your capacity to learn and absorb new information
is limitless as long as the *sponge* continues to grow.

The critical factor in becoming a *human sponge* is to use whatever information you have and constantly increase your thirst for more knowledge and greater understanding. Read a good book, take notes in the margins and think about how the principles in that book can be applied to increasing the quality of your life and of those around you. A book, a seminar, or a stimulating conversation can unlock a simple, yet profound key to exponentially increasing the quality of your *Journey*. Approach each day with a sense of growing excitement about what you can learn today. Whether it's a personal experience, a stimulating conversation, or anything else you take in through your five senses—all these events add to who you are and who you will become.

What can you consistently do to grow, learn, and evolve? There are four key areas of focus for building your skills as a *human sponge*:

Build a Library

Books and audio programs are vital components of the growth process. In five minutes or several hours you can engage in a stimulating discussion with some of the most extraordinary people of the present and past. And if you get just one new distinction or learn just one new thing, something that triggers your nervous system to take action, it's worth the time. But remember, the information is useless if you don't apply it in daily life.

There is more treasure in books than in all the pirates' loot on Treasure Island...and best of all, you can enjoy these riches every day of your life.
—Walt Disney

Keep a Journal

Record the process of your life. When you write freely, you discover things about yourself that you often overlook in your hurried pace through life. You uncover lessons that are right in front of your nose—lessons you neglect to see. Your journal is a place to capture your thoughts, experiences, and new lessons you learn each day. It's also a place to reflect on the day and once again give thanks and acknowledge how lucky you are to be alive. Another great practice is recording at least one new thing you've learned during the course of that day. This simple practice helps ensure you are measurably growing each day.

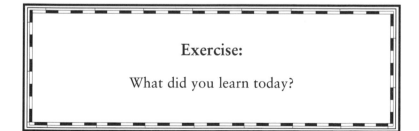

Exercise:

What did you learn today?

Take Seminars and Classes

It's mind-boggling to think that so many people believe the educational process stops after our formal education is finished. Granted that life's experiences are our greatest teachers, but why go unarmed into the battles of life? The more prepared we are, the greater chance we have of being victorious. There are specialized classes on almost anything, and most universities now offer continuing education classes. Also, for those who do not have access to such classes, the Internet provides an abundance of learning opportunities, often called "distant learning." (Distant learning courses have lectures over the Internet with home-study material.)

What sculpture is to a block of marble,
education is to the soul.
—Joseph Addison

Live Everyday Life

Lastly, and definitely most important, the arena of everyday life provides your greatest opportunity to learn and grow. Watch, question, listen and observe but also **ACT!** It is through your daily actions, failures, and experiences that you are able to achieve new levels of growth and understanding. *Go play and become a never-ending student of life!*

One of the biggest challenges in the educational system is that most students are not given an outlet to immediately use what they learn and therefore have a difficult time absorbing and growing from the educational process. Here lies the power of real-life experience—because you are forced to use what you learn and learn from your mistakes.

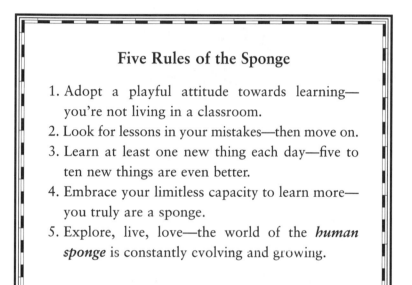

Five Rules of the Sponge

1. Adopt a playful attitude towards learning— you're not living in a classroom.
2. Look for lessons in your mistakes—then move on.
3. Learn at least one new thing each day—five to ten new things are even better.
4. Embrace your limitless capacity to learn more— you truly are a sponge.
5. Explore, live, love—the world of the *human sponge* is constantly evolving and growing.

The Education of Failure

A man's errors are his portals of discovery.
—James Joyce

The reason why many people never attempt the *Journey to the Impossible* is because they are afraid of making mistakes, of failing to succeed. This fear of making mistakes, which begins developing during childhood, hinders your ability to take action. Fear of failure can immobilize you, keeping you from taking any action and insuring that positive change remains an unattainable dream.

Your greatest growth comes from making mistakes. When you make mistakes you tend to reflect on what you have done. You ask questions that uncover invaluable lessons to increase your quality of life. And because you experience pain from the lesson the first time around, ideally, you apply the lesson immediately to create positive change. (I say "ideally" because many of us make the same mistake many times before learning the lesson.)

Instead of fearing mistakes and failure, get excited about them. If nothing else, this concept is confusing the heck out of your subconscious mind, and you will find yourself more eager to try new things. You should fear that you are not going to learn something—not that you are going to fail. In fact, real failure can only come when we cease learning and growing, so make mistakes often and learn quickly.

What is a recent "mistake" you made? What can you learn from it?

Ode

We are the music-makers,
 And we are the dreamers of dreams;
Wandering by lone sea-breakers,
 And sitting by desolate streams;
World-losers and world-forsakers,
 On whom the pale moon gleams;
Yet we are the movers and shakers,
 Of the world forever, it seems.

With wonderful deathless ditties
We build up the world's cities,
 And out of a fabulous story
 We fashion an empire's glory:
One man with a dream, at pleasure,
 Shall go forth and conquer a crown;
And three with a new song's measure
 Can trample an empire down.

We, in the ages lying
 In the buried past of the earth,
Built Nineveh with our sighing,
 And Babel itself with our mirth;
And o'erthrew them with prophesying
To the old of new world's worth;
For each age is a dream that is dying,
Or one that is coming to birth.

–Arthur O'Shaughnessy

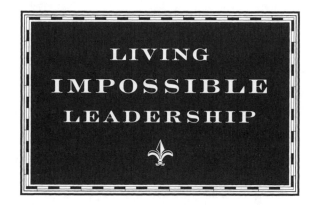

Defining Impossible Leadership

We need leaders of inspired idealism, leaders to whom are granted great visions, who dream greatly and strive to make their dreams come true, who can kindle the people with the fire from their burning souls.
—Theodore Roosevelt

Excessive use of the word leadership has dramatically diminished its value and power. Let us change that. What are the qualities that make a great leader? Is there a formula for cultivating leadership? What distinctions must you make to become an *Impossible Leader*?

There are two fundamental abilities required for *Impossible Leadership*:
    1. The ability to influence, inspire and motivate yourself
    2. The ability to influence, inspire and motivate others

The ability to influence yourself to create positive change in your own life is critical to becoming a dynamic leader. You know people watch what you do and not what you say. If you conduct your life inconsistently with what you preach, eventually you lose all credibility and positive influence over others. Think of any great leader in history, like Abraham Lincoln, Gandhi, or Martin Luther King, Jr.; their words matched their actions. People followed them.

There are four key roles we can use to further illustrate the qualities of an *Impossible Leader*:

The Influencer

We have already highlighted this concept above. Positive influence is a critical quality for all leaders—without it, leadership does not exist. The greater your level of influence, the higher the quality of people surrounding you and the greater the results you will produce. The *Influencer* is a talent hunter, he knows the more brilliant, passionate, and hungry the team, the better the results. The *Influencer* is a fierce negotiator who looks for win-win solutions that serve the team's needs. His compassion, respect, and understanding for people are astounding, and people love being around him.

The Visionary

The *Impossible Leader* is a *Visionary*, clear on where he (and his family, company, etc.) want to go. The *Visionary* stands tall with unshakable courage and certainty that he will make things happen. Others take comfort in the *Visionary's* certainty, believing he has an unusual power to take action and produce results. The *Visionary* is a rule breaker who goes against conventional thinking and procedures because of his clarity and conviction about the future he will create. His ability to innovate and anticipate the future puts him in a class of his own. The *Visionary* is in control of his destiny, responsible for his actions, and focused on getting results.

The Strategist

The *Impossible Leader* is a master *Strategist*, able to handle any problem and develop powerful plans of action. This tactician uses the creative faculties of his mind to find effective solutions and anticipate future challenges. He is a brilliant practitioner of fast and effective decision-making. The *Strategist* is constantly looking for ways to improve in all areas of his life. The *Strategist* follows guiding principles to produce consistent results that defy conventional beliefs and thinking.

The Explorer

The *Impossible Leader* is a true adventurer, exploring all the magnificent wonders on his *Journey to the Impossible*. The *Explorer* gives one hundred percent throughout the *Journey*—like a kid, he has fun, stays curious and constantly asks questions. He takes considerable risks and is not afraid of failure. In fact, he embraces failure as long as he finds a valuable lesson. As a student of life, he's always learning and growing—reading, listening, asking, attempting, failing—constantly expanding and evolving. When obstacles arise, the *Explorer* pioneers a path over, around, or through the belly of the beast.

23rd Century Leadership

It's in the moment of our decisions that our destiny is shaped.
—Anthony Robbins

"Make it so" were the immortal words of Jean-Luc Picard, Captain of the USS Enterprise in the late 2300s. This is a lesson in leadership. Have you ever seen any episodes of *Star Trek: The Next Generation*? The main role of the captain is to make quick and intelligent decisions—often based solely on the input of his crew. The captain taps into the vast knowledge base of his crew and then quickly makes a decision, giving the command with certainty. That is a key distinction. There are many situations in life where there are several difficult choices, and as a *Creator*, your team will look to you to steer them through.

In today's business environment, the time allowed for

critical decision-making has shrunk. If you edge forward with fear and uncertainty—right or wrong—you will likely lose. At the moment of decision, trust your ability to decide. Embody certainty in the face of insurmountable odds. You will train yourself to make consistent and quick intelligent decisions.

Analysis of over 25,000 men and women who had experienced failure disclosed the fact that lack of decision was near the head of the list of the thirty-one major causes of failure. Procrastination, the opposite of decision, is a common enemy that practically every man must conquer.
—Napoleon Hill

Seven Steps to Captain-Style Decision Making

1. Clarify the result/goal.
2. Quickly accumulate all necessary information.
3. Seek counsel to gain better understanding of the problem.
4. Brainstorm at least three possible options.
5. Evaluate all possible options based on desired results.
6. Make decisions with conviction.
7. Never doubt once the decision is made.

Keep in Mind

• Spend only 10 percent of your time on the problem and 90 percent of your time on finding a solution.
• Honor your ability to choose—be grateful for the power of choice.

Analysis of several hundred people who had accumulated fortunes well beyond the million–dollar mark disclosed the fact that every one of them had the habit of reaching decisions promptly, and of changing these decisions slowly, if, and when they were changed.
—Napoleon Hill

Own the Day!

The great end of life is not knowledge but action.
—*Thomas Henry Huxley*

If you don't, someone else will. If you neglect to take the day into your grasp and allow other people to seize the reins, you will be destined to a life of only meeting other people's demands and never having what you want. The *Journey to the Impossible* requires you to **own the day**, taking your destiny into your own hands.

What does it mean to **own the day**? The phrase sounds extremely similar to the infamous phrase *Carpe Diem* or *Seize the Day* but with one important distinction. When you **own the day**, you take responsibility—for your actions and for those you lead. When you **own it**, you take it inside and all your energy and drive work to make it happen.

When someone says, "I will **own** this project," you feel

certain it's going to get done—this person is demonstrating reassuring conviction and certainty. Too often, however, we do not take responsibility. We lay blame on other people or outside events and circumstances, letting the environment dictate what happens in our lives. Deep inside we are miserable and unfulfilled because of this.

As one on the *Journey*, wake up each morning and know you will take on the challenges of the day to build your empire. As a result of your relentless commitment to **owning the day**, others follow your lead. **Own the day** in every area of your life—with your family, your finances, your work, your relationships, and your emotional and physical well-being.

Remember the ball is always in your court. **So decide what you want to create and *own* the day!**

Apply yourself. Get all the education you can, but then, by God, do something. Don't just stand there, make it happen.
—Lee Iacocca

MAINTAINING
IMPOSSIBLE
HEALTH

From Sickness to Health

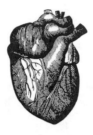

We can wax intellectual for days on end about the qualities, philosophies, and strategies you need to consistently make *impossible* things happen in our lives, but without our health, everything else is null and void. There's no point in having big plans for the future if you don't have the energy to *create* or if you're not even going to be around.

I was one of those kids who always got sick. Colds, fevers, strep throat, bad allergies—you name it, I had it often. And I was notorious for getting sick on or before important trips and events like vacations and holidays.

In first grade, I missed fifty days of school due to illnesses, and even in college I got, on average, five sinus infections each year. I remember having a skin test during college, where they pricked me sixty times around my back with a needle to determine what allergies I had—I was allergic to more than forty different things.

Following college, I introduced myself to a wide variety of exciting health principles by meeting a number of nutritional experts, attending a multitude of seminars and reading a huge selection of books on the topic.

Very quickly, I began making dramatic changes in my lifestyle—what I did and did not eat, what I drank, how I breathed, how I moved, and how I thought about my body and overall health. As I learned something new, I experimented with it for a while before determining whether or not it was useful for me. I kept what worked and discarded the rest.

Now, I am happy to report, I have not had any form of illness in more than four years (knock wood!)—not even a "common" cold. I feel healthy and full of energy on a consistent basis, and I haven't had to take any form of medication or over-the-counter drug.

Author's Note

There is so much information I want to share on this all-important topic of health, but space is limited. I would, however, implore you to aggressively seek out more information on health and energy principles, try stuff, keep what works and discard the rest. Many readers are already diligent students and practitioners of solid health principles—and I applaud you. For those who are not, there is still time—start right now. The reference guide in the back of this book, combined with the content of this chapter, will give you a terrific launching pad toward optimal health and energy.

Remember, your health is everything. Your *Journey* is dependent on your vessel of travel—your glorious body!

The Habit of Health

Not choice, but habit rules the unreflecting herd.
—William Wordsworth

The *World Health Organization* defines health as "a state of complete physical, mental, or social well-being, and not merely the absence of disease or infirmity." *Nutrition and Health Therapy* defines health as "optimal human fulfillment and productivity—quality of life." Both are accurate definitions, but let's define health as your body's ability to maintain a maximum reservoir of energy while functioning in a disease-free environment. Optimal energy allows you to make continual demands on your body. In other words, you need energy to do stuff. And I mean, serious energy, most likely more than you have ever been able to sustain.

We live in a toxic society where, for most of us, our staple source of "nourishment" can be purchased at a drive-through window. As a culture, we eat too much and exercise too little. We have become so "big-boned" as a society that statistics show that over 95 percent of Americans are overweight. As scary as that sounds, it gets worse. Being overweight dramatically increases your chances of getting life-threatening diseases by a factor of ten.

Here's a question: Why? Why are we digging our graves with our teeth? I wish I could say it's a lack of education, but I personally know too many overweight people who know how unhealthy and dangerous their weight is but who continue to eat as if there's going to be a famine tomorrow. I also can't say it's a lack of desire because there seems to be a new weight loss product on the market every other day, and there's no shortage of demand for them. People are constantly flocking to weight loss centers like Weight Watchers® and Jenny Craig®.

Perhaps it's a question of motivation, but I don't think that's the main issue. I believe the answer, albeit an unsexy one, is a matter of *habit*—habit combined with ineffective strategies and a disempowering mindset.

Most people never adopt the mindset of optimal energy. In order to **Create the Impossible** you often need to stay up late and wake up early, be in a peak emotional and physical state on a consistent basis and still have a reserve to turn up the intensity when necessary.

In the beginning of a new, exciting project, this is usually easy. In the early stages of the creation process, when you *tap into your fire* and you are beaming with unbridled passion and enthusiasm, you feel like you can take on the world. You feel like there are infinite reserves of energy within you and you go for it—full force. Eventually, however, your energy begins to dissipate, and if you do not allow your body sufficient time to recover, you become ill. (I know this pattern all too well from personal experience.) Either way, your *unstoppable momentum* is lost.

Learn the principles of energy, but more important, live them. Living in a state of vibrant health and energy unlocks the gateway to your desires.

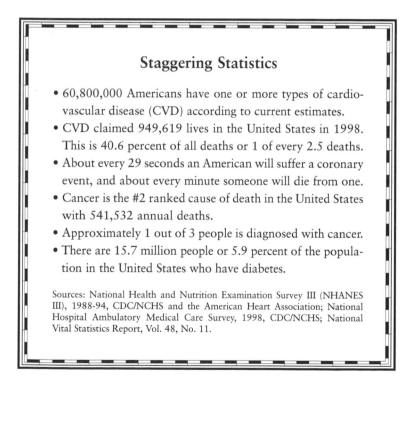

Staggering Statistics

- 60,800,000 Americans have one or more types of cardio-vascular disease (CVD) according to current estimates.
- CVD claimed 949,619 lives in the United States in 1998. This is 40.6 percent of all deaths or 1 of every 2.5 deaths.
- About every 29 seconds an American will suffer a coronary event, and about every minute someone will die from one.
- Cancer is the #2 ranked cause of death in the United States with 541,532 annual deaths.
- Approximately 1 out of 3 people is diagnosed with cancer.
- There are 15.7 million people or 5.9 percent of the population in the United States who have diabetes.

Sources: National Health and Nutrition Examination Survey III (NHANES III), 1988-94, CDC/NCHS and the American Heart Association; National Hospital Ambulatory Medical Care Survey, 1998, CDC/NCHS; National Vital Statistics Report, Vol. 48, No. 11.

The Six Pure Energy Principles

The first wealth is health.
—Ralph Waldo Emerson

To simplify our ***Journey*** to impossible levels of health, the following are the *six powerful principles of health and energy*. There is more detail about each principle on the pages that follow.

Pure Energy Principle #1 — Learn Health

Immerse yourself in information on health and energy. Adopt the discipline of constant growth in the area of health, live what you learn, keep what works and discard the rest.

Pure Energy Principle #2 — Breathe for Life

The quality of your life is in large part a function of the quality of your breathing. Learn to breathe deeply, using your diaphragm, the way you did when you were a baby, and tap into your body's true power.

Pure Energy Principle #3 — Eat to Energize

Eat the foods that fuel your body and nourish your cells. Avoid the foods that poison your body and your blood. The principle of *Eat to Energize* is important for achieving ***impossible results*** in any area of your life.

Pure Energy Principle #4 — Hydrate Like Crazy

Water is the source of life and the key to increasing and sustaining high levels of energy. Drink quality water throughout the day to support your body's proper functioning. *Water is a more powerful and sustainable source of energy than caffeine.*

Pure Energy Principle #5 — Exercise For Life

Incorporate aerobic activity into your everyday life and feel the gift of physical power and vitality. Thirty minutes of aerobic exercise at your target heart rate will help maintain a higher quality of life.

Pure Energy Principle #6 — Master Your Mind

The mind has the ability to heal and the ability to make ill. A directed mind is critical for the creation and maintenance of optimal health and energy.

It's a Matter of Lifestyle

Don't go on a diet; change your life. Don't "take up" exercise; change your life. "Diets" rarely last—they are temporary objectives for the moment that do not set up an environment for living a vibrant life with boundless energy. When you adopt a new lifestyle—with a new commitment to proper eating, breathing, exercise, etc.—you change your way of thinking, and your life changes forever.

Adopt a passion for energy.

Pure Energy Principle 1: Learn Health

When it comes to your health, you can never know too much. Learn how your body works and how you can promote greater levels of energy. There's no definitive authority on health—the field is flooded with experts on specific areas of health—and new advances and theories are always being discovered. Become a scientist for your own body, and you will find what works for you.

Read, or should I say, consume as many books and magazines as you can on different health information and practices. Keep a healthy curiosity while you seek out what works for you.

To create amazing levels of health and energy necessary for your *Journey*, continually stretch yourself. Resolve to develop unparalleled standards of health in your daily life. Your health is everything—without it, you have nothing.

Health Education is Empowering for Three Reasons:

1. The more you understand about how your body functions, the easier it is for you to determine what lifestyle changes you want to make.
2. When you understand what foods are harmful and what they do to your body, it is easier not to consume them.
3. The more information you have, the more empowered you will be and the greater positive impact you can have in educating those around you.

Pure Energy Principle 2: Breathe for Life

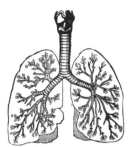

Breathing is an involuntary action that we must learn to do consciously and effectively. But we all know how to breathe, right? Actually, we all use to know. Have you ever watched a baby breathe? A baby's stomach expands and contracts in a very peaceful and natural movement.

Think about how you are breathing right now. In fact, try this: Take a deep breath with a big inhale, followed by a long exhale. Okay, what did you do? Did you allow your stomach to expand and fill with air as you inhaled? Or did you breathe with your chest, expanding and raising your chest while inhaling and dropping it while exhaling? Most people breathe with their chests, which collapses their lungs, rendering them unable to fill with air.

Athletes, babies, and all those on the *Journey* to greater

energy and vitality learn to breathe diaphragmatically. The diaphragm is the layer of muscle that separates the chest cavity from the abdominal cavity. When you breathe diaphragmatically, your diaphragm contracts and your stomach (i.e. abdomen) sticks out, allowing your lungs to expand and fill with air.

Deep diaphragmatic breathing is critical for creating high levels of health and energy because it helps oxygenate our blood cells. Oxygen is the source of all energy in our bodies. Breathing diaphragmatically consistently will increase your level of energy throughout the day.

Exercise: The Right Breath

To practice diaphragmatic breathing, place your hands on your stomach, right above your waist. Take a long deep breath, imagining that you are filling a big balloon resting in the pit of your stomach (expanding your stomach). When you exhale, imagine the air deflating from the balloon (contracting your stomach). By practicing this simple exercise three times a day for four weeks, you will help to condition yourself to breathe life and energy into your body and, consequently, into everything you do.

Pure Energy Principle 3: Eat to Energize

This one fundamental distinction can change your life forever! You can transform the quality of life by eating the foods that provide your body with the fuel needed not only to live disease-free but also to feel energized every day.

Eating an energizing diet, which includes eating many different green and other vegetables, sprouted grains, and even certain oils, is a challenge for many people. They are use to eating the foods they were brought up on, which unfortunately, do not support the body's proper functions. If, however, you shift your focus from eating what you're used to and what may feel good for the moment to what's going to give you more energy, you will receive amazing rewards.

A key element to energizing your body is eating the proper proportion of water-rich foods. Our bodies are made up of approximately seventy percent water. It is logical that seventy percent of our food intake should be foods with high water content, like vegetables. Maintaining an energizing diet usually means eating considerably more vegetables than you are currently eating. Try this for ten days. Stay conscious of any changes in your sleeping patterns and energy level. The amount of energy you can sustain when your body is able to quickly digest and metabolize all the food you are ingesting is staggering.

If you stay conscious of your eating and learn to be in tune with your body, you'll find it easier to determine which foods support your body's proper functioning and which foods do not. Here's a list of energizing and energy-draining foods to help get you started on your *Journey* to an energized way of life.

Energizing Foods Include:

Almonds, asparagus, avocados, broccoli, brussels sprouts, carrots, cauliflower, celery, cucumbers, dates, green beans, green leafy vegetables, lemons, limes, peppers (all colors), radishes, spinach, sprouted seeds and grains, tomatoes, walnuts, wheat grass

Energy-Draining Foods Include:

Beef, beer, butter, coffee, chicken, cottage cheese, hot dogs, lobster, margarine, milk, pork, refined sugar, shrimp, sour cream, turkey, veal, white bread

Eat Less

They are as sick that surfeit with too much,
as they that starve with nothing.
—William Shakespeare

If you truly want to embrace an **Impossible Journey**, consume smaller amounts of food—very likely a fraction of what you currently consume.

Remember, *food is fuel*—that's why we eat. We are eating to live, not living to eat. Too often we forget this fact, and we eat until there is nothing in sight, including an ounce of strength to get up from the table.

I come from a family that loves to eat, where food is a cross between a lifelong passion and an Olympic sport. My grandmother is never content until all the food from the table is eaten, and she always makes enough food for twice as many people as are coming to dinner. I can't recall a meal at my grandparent's house where I didn't have trouble breathing comfortably after a meal.

Be conscious of your body while you eat and notice when you are satiated—then stop. Once you train your body and mind to adopt the principles of health, you'll find that you'll naturally eat less and feel hungry less.

Your Body is Your Temple

Do you not know that your body is a temple of the Holy Spirit, who is in you, whom you have received from God? You are not your own; you were bought at a price. Therefore honor God with your body.
—I Corinthian 6:19-20

For the *Journey*, we need to be able to harness massive reserves of energy and greatly minimize our needed recovery time. This is where the *Creator's* mindset comes in. Understand, believe and know that your body, or should I say, your *temple*, is an incredible gift and unless you come to honor that gift, your ability to create will be limited.

Would you deface your temple by throwing garbage into it? (i.e. fast food and other poisonous foods and substances.) Or would you treat your temple in such a caring way that it could be around forever?

Pure Energy Principle 4: Hydrate Like Crazy

This principle has created a big shift in the quality of my life. In college, I spent pretty much all of my time in one of the local coffee shops, and coffee and tea became my primary sources of nourishment. (I once did the equivalent of nine expresso shots in a day—it wasn't pretty—my body was actually vibrating the table from shaking.)

Water is a critical component to all living matter, and the human body is made up of around seventy percent of this life-giving element. All of the body's basic and essential functions like digestion, circulation, and excretion require water. Water plays an important role in the body's metabolism, nutrient transport, and proper cell functions.

The challenge is most of us live in an almost constant state of dehydration. Pure water is imperative for hydration—

other liquids containing water, like tea, coffee, alcohol, and manufactured beverages, contain dehydrating agents. Most people think they're only dehydrated when they get thirsty or their mouth gets dry. Doctor Fereydoon Batmanghelidj, medical researcher and author of *Your Body's Many Cries for Water*, says that dry mouth is the **last** signal of dehydration of the body.

If you just adhere to this one principle of constantly hydrating your body, with mountain or spring water particularly, you'll be amazed at the results. In addition to having more energy, you'll also find you get hungry less frequently.

How Much Water Should You Drink?

A good general rule of thumb is to drink half your body weight in ounces each day. For example, if you weigh 140 pounds, you should drink 70 ounces of water per day.

Also, avoid drinking any liquids during and directly after meals; doing so hinders proper digestion and does not provide any energy-related benefits. (Wait at least one hour after meals.)

Pure Energy Principle 5: Exercise for Life

We all know that exercise is important, but many of us don't know why. Aerobic exercise, sustained movement over a period of time, provides your body with the energy you need to thrive and build momentum. Aerobic exercise helps increase your body's oxygen supply (*aerobic* literally means *with oxygen*), which helps support the rest of your body's functions. Among the many benefits, aerobic training helps lower your resting heart rate, helps with digestion, allows for easier blood flow and helps your lungs operate more efficiently.

The key to effectively living the *Exercise for Life* energy principle is to find a form of aerobic exercise you enjoy. Generally speaking, aerobic activities require a relatively lower heart rate (compared to anaerobic activities, exercise that is performed at higher levels of intensity) and can include jogging, bicycling, swimming, hiking, dancing, and skating. An exercise is aerobic or anaerobic, depending on the rate at which your heart is beating (see *Your Ideal Heart Rate* on the next page). For example, a casual aerobic bike ride can become anaerobic if you exert yourself too hard, causing shortness of breath and fatigue.

I used to go through vicious cycles of exercising hard for a period of about twenty days, and then I'd stop. I would make myself crazy, pushing myself until I was totally exhausted— and for the next several days the pain and soreness made it difficult to move, literally. The excessive anaerobic exercising I was doing, like running hard for thirty minutes when my body wasn't use to it, was actually causing prolonged fatigue and physical injuries.

By learning to perform aerobic activities at your target heart rate, you can maximize the benefits of your training, limit the risk of physical injury, and have a lot more fun in the process. What is your target heart rate?

Your Ideal Aerobic Heart Rate

The key to proper aerobic activity is to perform any exercise at your ideal heart rate. Your ideal heart rate for aerobic training can be estimated by subtracting your age from 180. For example, if you're 35-years-old, your target heart rate for aerobic training is probably around 145. You may need to add or subtract from that rate depending on the amount of time you've been exercising and on your overall physical condition. Warm-up and cooldown rates are also important in conducting an effective aerobic activity.

A fitness trainer can help you better determine your ideal rate hearts for aerobic training and burning fat, but the above rule of thumb will help.

Pure Energy Principle 6: Master Your Mind

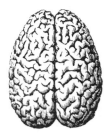

The greatest mistake physicians make is that they attempt to cure the body without attempting to cure the mind; yet the mind and body are one and should not be treated separately!
—Plato

It's a funny thing. You can do almost everything right—eat right, exercise, breath, stretch, drink lots of water, etc.—and still have low energy, little endurance, and a high propensity for illness and feel generally lousy.

There is one final principle for living a life of vibrant health and energy. This component is called ***mindful mastery***—the ability to master your mental focus and direction. Without this mastery you will continually experience pain, and with it you can experience the joy and bliss that come from taking control of your life.

After having been living the other *pure energy principles* of health and vitality for over two years, I still felt completely lethargic at times. I was getting adult acne, and I was waking up tired no matter how much sleep I had. I was eating mostly water-rich foods and living the other principles of health, but I had recently put my second business startup venture on hold because of financial challenges. I was deep into credit card debt, and I had zero income. I was still exercising and eating correctly, yet I felt terrible. I was in a constant state of lethargy.

I was aware of my poor mental state and would frequently snap out of it but usually I'd fall right back, feeling helpless, alone, tired, and confused. I was not directing my mind. Needless to say, I was not in a resourceful state.

Now I could have said, "Well, I guess this health stuff is bull. I have no energy living this way. I might as well give up and eat everything." But luckily, I was smarter than that. I knew what needed to change—it was not what I was feeding my body, but rather, what I was feeding my mind. I was focusing on what I didn't have instead of being thankful for what I did have, which was leading to stress and a poor state of health.

The first step to achieving *mindful mastery*: Be grateful for life. Next, get clear about what you really want and why you want it. Is it a burning desire? Are you willing to do whatever it takes? What's it worth to you? Continue asking quality questions, expecting quality answers.

After answering these questions, you will feel your energy skyrocket as your level of passion, joy, and enthusiasm increase in direct proportion to your energy. You will be able to work around the clock on a high you would not believe. Haven't you had this feeling—where you were so excited about an event that you couldn't sleep (and you didn't want to sleep) and you seemed to have boundless energy? Wouldn't it be great if you could live that way on a daily basis?

Impossible, you say? Well, isn't that what this is all about? Okay, so it's *impossible* to feel the excitement, to experience limitless energy and happiness on a consistent basis. Well, why not just do it anyway?

Those who keep the peace of their inner selves
in the midst of the tumult of the modern city
are immune from nervous diseases.
—Dr. Alexis Carrel

Rejuvenation Days

One of my favorite practices that has yielded immeasurable returns consistently is taking *rejuvenation days*. A *rejuvenation day* is a day or block of time that is consciously set aside to nurturing your body, mind, and soul. This period of rest and recovery is critical in your pursuit to achieving incredible results for several reasons.

First, periods of rejuvenation recharge your body with the energy needed to attain desired results. In your pursuit of the unthinkable, you often overextend yourself, depleting your physical and mental energy, which eventually leads to burn out. I started taking *rejuvenation days* because I found myself continually falling prey to this overexertion.

Second, when you are clear on your purpose and your vision for the future, your intensity increases as you discover more ways to turn your dreams into a physical reality. Your pursuit can become stale unless you allow your mind to decompress during a rejuvenation cycle. This may appear counterintuitive but the best way to stay on target is to periodically take a step back and clear your head.

Third, taking a *rejuvenation day* will enhance your creative thinking as you rebuild your body and mind into a highly resourceful state. You will be amazed at the ideas and connections you will make after taking a day to ***just be***.

Finally, *rejuvenation days* are fun! These days are designed solely around what you want to do.

Guidelines for the Day

Here are a few useful guidelines and suggestions for maximizing your rejuvenation experience:

1. At least a portion (if not all) of the time spent on these days should be spent alone. Remember, the purpose of these days is to clear your mind, and mindless chattering with a friend is usually not the best way to achieve this outcome. (At times, spending time with your friends or family can be highly rejuvenating.)

2. Immerse yourself in nature. This goes for hikers and non-hikers alike. There is something amazingly rejuvenating about being in nature—breathing the air, observing the flora and fauna, walking on dirt paths. Even if you live in the most metropolitan cities in the world, you can still find a natural place to energize—thank God for Central Park!

3. Pack a bag. Treat the day as a mini adventure. Take whatever items you might need on this adventure: a great book, a journal, a blanket or towel, water, a few snacks and whatever else you deem essential travel items.

4. Take a rejuvenation hour. Sometimes our demanding schedules do not allow us an entire day for energizing the soul—pulling yourself away from your work and taking an hour to *just be* can be enough to recharge you.

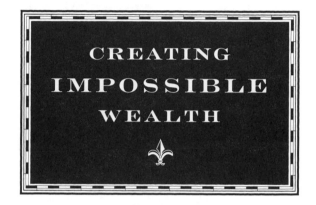

CREATING
IMPOSSIBLE
WEALTH

What is Money?

What a profound question. Money is rectangular green paper with pictures of deceased notables. Sure, in the United States, that is true. Money is legal tender for all debts, public and private. That is true too, though I don't find either of these definitions very useful.

Money is a form of energy. Money represents an exchange of value—in order to make money, you need to add value. If you integrate this understanding of money into your daily life, your finances can dramatically change. If you already have this belief, you know what I mean.

Money, wealth, and abundance are challenging issues for many people. Some people think money is not important or money is evil. This is not very intuitive because money is just energy—neither good nor evil. What a person does with money is another story, but little green paper is not the cause.

The more money you have, the greater positive impact you can have on the world. You can create empowering beliefs about money, or you can be poor. What do you choose?

Wealth Building 101

'My other piece of advice, Copperfield,' said Mr. Micawber,
'you know. Annual income twenty pounds, annual expenditure
nineteen nineteen six, results happiness. Annual income twenty
pounds, annual expenditure twenty pounds ought and six,
results misery. The blossom is blighted, the leaf is withered, the
God of day goes down upon the dreary scene, and—and in
short you are for ever floored. As I am!'
—Charles Dickens

Unfortunately, to my knowledge, there aren't any high
school or university-level courses with this title. Since grad-
uating from college, I have become entranced and passionate
about how one creates wealth—in abundance. So few people
have achieved this feat, and I have always been fascinated
with the mysteries of wealth creation. Reading the yearly issue

of the *Forbes 400 Richest Americans* always got me excited then very frustrated. What did these people know? More importantly, what did these people do differently than everyone else?

I resolved to uncover the mystery behind wealth creation and began devouring any and all the books I could find on wealth building and personal finance. I took courses on trading and investing in the financial markets. I learned how to trade options and build a stock portfolio. I went to seminars on tax strategies and took classes on small business management. I started several different companies, meeting with investors and networking with fellow entrepreneurs. I went to conferences and heard keynote addresses by incredibly powerful and wealthy CEOs and other business executives. When I was around affluent people, I watched closely what they did and how they conducted their lives.

Yet still, I was poor. In fact, my debt was getting out of hand, and I was getting dizzy trying to juggle so many credit cards. I was getting more and more angry at my financial situation. My pain forced me to take a step back for a moment and reevaluate my predicament. Becoming unemotional about the issue, I noticed that although I had been reading and observing all this stuff about making money and creating wealth, I was not *doing* any of it! I was both shocked and appalled by this fact.

I committed to doing three things immediately to begin turning my finances around. These three actions are not new, are overly simplistic and are readily available—yet they remain a mystery to most people. Once one takes action on these ideas, the secrets of creating wealth are fully revealed, paving the way to a very prosperous life.

Warning: At this point it is important to take note of something. One must not be thrown off by the simplicity of these ideas. Remember, you never went through *Wealth Building 101*. A strong foundation will enable you to build the fortune you seek. Unless you are currently applying each principle, you cannot fully know the secrets nor can you create wealth.

Action #1: Stop the Bleeding

The first fundamental for building a strong financial foundation is to spend less than you earn. Most people do not do this. Credit cards are a big reason for this but the responsibility falls on the person owning the credit card, not the card itself. If you do not stop the financial hemorrhaging, wealth will always evade you.

Action #2: Save Like a Champ

You must put away at least ten percent of what you earn, but ideally substantially more than ten percent. This money needs to be put away to grow on its own, a force working for you even while you sleep. The amount may seem insignificant at first but it can continue to grow through the power of compounding interest, exponentially growing to reach staggering levels over time. Use a direct transfer mechanism from your checking account to avoid the monthly haste and thought process of making the transaction.

Action #3: Set Your Targets

If you don't know where you want to go, you probably will never get there. Most people never create specific financial objectives. Instead, they focus on what's not working, and all the negative things they don't want. To build a solid foundation, set targets and fire away. Create a plan and go to work.

Lastly, if you have not read *Think and Grow Rich* by Napoleon Hill, go read it now. And if you have, read it again. Actually, don't just read this book, live it.

*The Wealthy focus on **creating** more.*
*The Poor focus on **protecting** what they have.*

*The Wealthy operate from a position of **power**.*
*The Poor operate from a position of **fear**.*

Seven Wealth Clues

We should be glad of an opportunity to serve others by any invention of ours and this we should do freely and generously.
—Benjamin Franklin

In a study of wealth creation, it is logical to look at those who have been successful at this craft and find ways to duplicate what they do. In making such observations, you uncover **seven clues** that guide the creation of wealth. People from all walks of life, regardless of their current socio-economic conditions or any past experiences, can apply these **seven wealth clues**. These **clues** are subtle and simplistic, though elusive to many people. The *common sense* needed to fully understand and apply these principles is apparently not very common.

You may read about these *clues* in a book or magazine or hear someone discussing them at the next table in a fine restaurant or in a great movie. In fact, it's possible that you have heard or seen these *clues* dozens or hundreds of times throughout your life, but unless you consciously apply these *seven wealth clues,* they are of little value to you.

Should you choose to thoroughly apply these principles in your own life, however, the changes that will take place are assured to be magnificent. But it is apparent that not everyone holds this belief because many people are too afraid of failing to apply these principles. What a shame, for it is one thing to go through life ignorant of the existence of these wealth clues, but it is ludicrous to know of their existence and still take little or no action.

The following *seven wealth clues* can lead you to all the *impossible wealth* you desire. Read them, study them, but most importantly, apply them.

Wealth Clue #1: No Retreat, No Surrender

The wealthy always leave little or no room for escape, putting everything on the line—do or die. They are used to *burning all bridges of escape,* never willing to retreat. They seem to always have this burning look in their eyes—a look of total conviction and certainty they will find a way.

Wealth Clue #2: Let It Ride

The wealthy are *willing to lose big* to get to the next level, never getting too comfortable or attached to what they have. The level of risk they are willing to take makes most people queasy and nauseous. Richard Branson sold his "baby," Virgin Records, to fuel a bigger vision in Virgin Atlantic Airline. Everyone said it would fail; now it is one of the best airlines in the world.

Wealth Clue #3: Rule Breaker, Rule Maker

The wealthy are *rule breakers by necessity*, because you cannot create wealth if you follow the rules of the masses— the masses are poor! The wealthy do not get caught up with what "everybody else" is doing—they are too busy working to pull off there own victories.

Wealth Clue #4: Step Up And Turn on the Juice

The wealthy seem to always have the energy to go non-stop, especially when everyone else goes home. I have noticed that most wealthy people are always ready to go and have an uncanny ability to *turn it on* when necessary. One of the main reasons for this phenomenon is that truly wealthy people do what they love. Hence, they rarely feel like they are working—work is play.

Wealth Clue #5: Treasure Hunting

The wealthy are always treasure hunting, constantly on the prowl for new opportunities, ready to jump on them as soon as they arise. This *opportunity consciousness* allows the wealthy to attract and identify hidden value no one else can find. Like a child getting a new toy, these treasure hunters take immense joy in the evaluation and evolution of a new idea. It's the people who have so much on their plate that are always looking for more.

Wealth Clue #6: Ownership and Responsibility

The wealthy always work for themselves because they must *have ownership* of the decision-making process within their businesses, thereby shaping their destiny. Consequently, they also *take responsibility* for what happens to their personal and professional life, never blaming anyone else, taking full ownership of all mishaps and sharing in all the victories with their team.

Wealth Clue #7: A Directed Mind

The wealthy understand that *thoughts are things* and that to create what you want, you must put all your energy in focus toward your goal. They understand that negative thoughts have the power to destroy, just as positive thoughts have the ability to create. By visualizing what they desire, the wealthy consistently find ways to move closer to getting what they want—no matter what obstacles are presented.

Strategies of the Poor

It is the mind that maketh good or ill,
that maketh wretch or happy, rich or poor.
—Edmund Spenser

Just as there are clues to what the wealthy do, there are clues to what the poor do. There are specific actions and thought processes that guarantee a life of financial ruin. The challenge is these actions and thoughts are usually present by default. Without constant and consistent action toward what you want, these *strategies of the poor* show up at your door.

The purpose of this section is not to reprimand those who struggle financially. The purpose is to communicate a set of observations so we are aware of what may be hindering the pursuit of wealth. If you know someone who is struggling financially, most likely they are subconsciously applying these *strategies of the poor.* By being aware of the existence and application of these *strategies* in our lives and in the lives of others, we gain the power to make conscious decisions and adopt the strategies of the rich. (Read the *Seven Wealth Clues* in the previous section.)

The *strategies of the poor* provide valuable insight into what **not** to do in the pursuit of *impossible wealth*:

Strategy #1: Lack of Focus

The poor *focus on what they don't want,* instead of what they do want. They complain about things being too expensive, about having too much debt, and having too little energy. The poor never know what they really want but are very specific about what they don't want. Because they never train their thinking to focus on what they truly desire, the poor usually stay poor.

Strategy #2: Who's to Blame?

The poor blame other people or other things for how things turn out. They blame society, their parents, their schooling, and their job. The poor *never take responsibility* for their own actions nor the circumstances of their life. As such, they live life in a completely disempowering state, unable to create a life of greater fulfillment.

Strategy #3: The Value of Time

The poor *spend their time wasting time.* They get bored on a regular basis and fill most of their "free time" with non-growth related activities. The poor go to a job while the wealthy build a fortune. The poor are not focused on adding value and usually have no sense of urgency to make something happen. The wealthy invest their time; the poor waste their time.

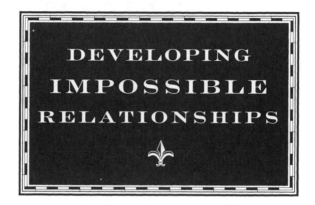

DEVELOPING
IMPOSSIBLE
RELATIONSHIPS

The Most Important Relationship of All

Know thyself.
—Plato

Are you intrigued? Can you feel the suspense? Oh, the anticipation. I just can't take it anymore. The most important relationship of all, outside the one with your Creator, is not with your spouse or "significant other," it's not with your children and it's not with your friends—that's right, it's with *yourself*. If you don't learn to master your communication with yourself, you will never be able to master your communication with anyone else.

How in touch are you with your emotional states on a daily basis? Do you know how you will react in any given situation? Are you crystal clear about what you want? Do you know what type of personality you have? Do you know what your belief system is about life, love, happiness, money, or relationships? Do you know what's most important to you in life? If you get stressed, do you know how to get yourself out of stress quickly?

It's lunacy to focus on communicating with other people before you learn to communicate and understand yourself. Get clear about who you are now and who you want to become in the future. Constantly strive to learn more about yourself and learn how to master your emotions.

Once this all-powerful relationship is in order, you will find your other important relationships will fall into place more easily. It is only after you learn to truly know yourself and appreciate who you are that you can fully open up and embrace those you love and care about. Many people try so hard to love other people without ever loving themselves. The *Journey* starts within. Begin consciously and openly communicating and loving yourself—watch the effect it has on all your other relationships.

To thine own self be true.
—William Shakespeare

Understanding You

Here are a few questions to help you master your communication with yourself:

1. When a challenge arises, what do you say to yourself?
2. How do you react in times of stress?
3. What has to happen for you to feel happy? Love? Lucky? Excited?
4. What has to happen for you to feel sad? Depressed? Angry?
5. What is most important to you in life?

Become an Empath

Be kind, for everyone you meet is fighting a hard battle.
—Plato

One of the fundamental skills you must master on your way to getting what you want is communication procedures of an *Empath*. Empathy is defined by *Webster's* as the projection of one's own personality into the personality of another in order to understand him better. *Empaths* from *Star Trek: The Next Generation* are a race of beings called Betazoids, who have the innate ability to read others' thoughts and emotions. An *Empath*, then, is someone who has the ability to fully connect and associate with another human being. An *Empath* builds instant rapport with people, connects with them on the deepest level and operates from a place of loving compassion. An *Empath* is influential, persuasive, and charismatic.

The secret of an *Empath* is his love and compassion for people and his ability to actively listen to words, voice, and body language. To become an *Empath*, one must strive for total understanding and want to help and contribute. Without contributing, you will never be able to connect completely with anyone or become a person of positive influence. This focus on giving to others will not only have a dramatic effect on how you communicate with others but will also have an even greater effect on how you feel.

Key Practices of an Empath

- An *Empath* smiles often, knowing that smiles are contagious.
- An *Empath* makes sure to look everyone he encounters (including servers in restaurants, grocery stores, gas stations, etc.) right in the eyes and give a warm "thank you."
- An *Empath* completely focuses on what the other person is saying, instead of thinking about what to say next.
- An *Empath* serves others, honoring every human being he meets as a gifted individual.

Beginning today, treat everyone you meet as if they were going to be dead by midnight. Extend to them all the care, kindness, and understanding you can muster, and do it with no thought of any reward. Your life will never be the same again.
—Og Mandino

Self-Evaluation

Men suffer all their lives under the foolish superstition
that they can be cheated. But it is impossible for a man
to be cheated by anyone but himself.
—Ralph Waldo Emerson

In striving to achieve our goals, we often become so focused on what we want that we neglect to be honest about where we are right now. Being honest with yourself is often a great challenge when you are striving to achieve the *impossible*. It's not always easy facing up to where you are now in a troublesome area of your life. A person will say he wants to create incredible financial wealth, but then he is not honest about the growing debt and lack of wealth strategies he has right now. If you are not honest with your-self, you will not be able to create what you want in your life. And if, for example, your finances are an area of focus for you, you have to be honest about where you are or all your efforts to create change will not come to pass. It can be painful being brutally honest with yourself because you may have been living a lie for so long that the situation (e.g., your finances) is totally out of control. That will change—but only after you acknowledge where you are.

The language you use is also critical for clearly evaluating where you are. There is an enormous difference between being a little overweight and being too fat to fit through a door. There is a huge difference between having relationship issues and being one step away from divorce. There is a monstrous difference between having some credit card debt and doing "plastic surgery" with six credit cards, with finance charges that equal or exceed your current income.

Exercise: Self-Evaluation

Is there an area (or areas) of your life about which you are not being totally honest with yourself? Write down how it really is—don't make it worse than it is, just be honest.

The Mentor's Gift

Keep away from people who try to belittle your ambitions.
Small people do that, but the really great make you feel that
you, too, can become someone great.
—Mark Twain

Throughout the history of storytelling, an essential character, the wise mentor, supported every great hero. Think back to any great cinematic adventure—Yoda and Luke Skywalker in *Star Wars*, Merlin and King Arthur in the tales of Camelot or, more recently, Morpheus and Neo in *The Matrix*. There's always a powerful teacher/student relationship driving the hero forward on his quest for self-discovery and victory. Of course not every story has such clearly defined mentoring roles, but they do generally exist.

Understand that the answer you seek is usually within

you. The role of the mentor is to help uncover that which, deep down, you already know.

You need a mentor. In fact, you may need many mentors. These sacred souls from all walks of life can help guide your *Journey* to creating the unimaginable. Now, I don't want you to go run out and find some guru in India or a mystic in Nepal—a guru is not a mentor.

A mentor is someone who listens, supports and encourages you, providing valuable insight from his or her personal experiences. There are wonderful mentors all around you. You may find a mentor in a parent, a friend, a family member, or the guy who pours you coffee in a coffee shop. There are people you can learn from, who can help guide your decision-making process and help you grow as a human being.

You may be saying to yourself, "But I have no mentors. There's no one around me I can turn to." Okay, that may, in fact, be true—what then? Go find one! Stay conscious that you are looking for a mentor, think about where you may find him and be patient. There's an old saying, "When the student is ready, the teacher appears." Stay ready and aware—you never know where you will find your mentor. The process of finding a mentor can be challenging because there are no rules and neither you nor your future mentor may be aware of the connection when you meet. You may discover that your mentor was right there all along. You just didn't allow yourself to see him or her.

Be Coachable

In order to develop a powerful mentoring relationship, commit to being *coachable*—be open, willing to learn with the curiosity of an excited kid. Do not judge or bring too much ego into any relationship. Be coachable not only in your mentoring relationships, but in life!

The mentoring relationship is built on trust and respect—without these two qualities, the relationship cannot grow and flourish. Remember, you have picked your mentor because he possesses qualities and abilities you wish to learn. Make certain you are fully willing to listen and learn. Both you and your mentor will learn invaluable lessons from each other as long as both players remain coachable and eager to grow.

Inherently, each one of us has the substance within to achieve whatever our goals and dreams define. What is missing from each of us is the training, education, knowledge, and insight to utilize what we already have.
—Mark Twain

Final Note on Mentoring

Perhaps the best way to find a mentor while getting an immense sense of contribution and fulfillment is to first become a mentor yourself. Find someone who can use additional support or just a friend. You can find your mentee in a little brother or sister, a next-door neighbor or someone you play sports with—people in need are all around you.

You can also join a mentorship program, mentoring a teenager on an ongoing basis. For more information visit the National Mentorship Partnership website:

www.mentoring.org

CONQUERING
IMPOSSIBLE
CHALLENGES

The Challenge

It's easy to celebrate when things are going in your favor.
It's easy to acknowledge your efforts when you're winning.
It's easy to feel good when you are already feeling good.

The challenge comes in celebrating each day
regardless of the event.
The challenge comes in breaking through
the day-to-day monotonies and mundane tasks.
The real challenge is to feel good
when you have so many reasons to feel bad.

To conquer these challenges is to achieve mastery
in your own life.
To conquer these challenges is to live
a happy and fulfilled life...
a life of purpose.

–Scott Jeffrey

Invincible Courage

Courage in danger is half the battle.
—Plautus

Your *Journey to the Impossible* will be painful at times. You may want to quit and give up, following the path of the status quo. You will be tired, worn out, physically beat up, and emotionally exhausted. You may even want to cry now and then (and that's okay). Remember, it is these challenging times that require you to grow, stretch yourself and move forward. When you are exhausted, push a little harder. When you are in pain, do a little more. When you feel like giving up, break through your fears and celebrate on your chosen path. Very simply, possess *invincible courage*.

You are one in a select few, a member of a group that knows there is more to life than you are currently experiencing—that a more fulfilling level of life always exists. Most people would not read the book you are holding in your hands, and even less would reach this far in the text. The concept of a *Journey to the Impossible* would be incredulous to these nonbelievers. They use a dialect foreign to all **Impossibility Seekers**—phrases such as:

"But that's impossible."
"You can't do that."
"Who are you kidding?"
"Why even bother trying?"
"It'll never work."
"Might as well give up."
"Call it quits."
"But it has always been this way."
"I always mess up."
"I never win, I'm just not lucky."

Creators of the Impossible move forward when others retreat. Your courage allows you to think differently than most people, to not take most things as givens and to **ACT**. Your *courage* keeps you up late at night and gets you up early. Your courage allows you to conduct your life with higher standards and higher ideals, and consequently, you achieve greater results.

Those on the *Journey* must be prepared to stand alone—to break away from the comfort and familiarity of the crowd. This is a terribly frightening thought to many people who would rather be unhappy but secure, rather than leading an extraordinary life with a smaller group, the courageous few.

You can't cross the sea merely by staring at the water.
—Rabindranath Tagore

The Rewards of Courage

You get to be fulfilled mentally, emotionally, spiritually, socially, and financially. You get all the rewards that life has to offer. You get to know you are capable of anything, that you can conquer any challenge and can stand alone. You become an even more extraordinary being than you are now because of the immense growth and contribution you experience along the way. You get all the joy, happiness, faith, gratitude, passion, strength, and energy that you can handle. You get to experience abundance in all areas of your life. Get the picture?

Is it worth the challenging road ahead? Are you willing to tap into levels of courage within yourself that until now may have been dormant? I can hear you saying, "YES!"

Move the Rock

*"When you get into a tight place and it seems you can't go
on...hold on, for that's just the place and the time
when the tide will turn."*
—Harriet Beecher Stowe

Along your *Journey to the Impossible*, inevitably you
are going to go through those times when you feel like
there's no place left to go. Do this: Get excited! What?
That's right; get excited because the unimaginable is about
to happen.

There are two options when caught between a rock and
a hard place. You can **move the rock** or **blow through the
hard place**. That's it. The above strategies are the keys to
your doorway to the *impossible life*. The power you harness when you use these two strategies will change your life
forever.

The pain of a precarious situation causes most people to instinctively retreat. Fearful souls escape in many ways, either by eating excessively, watching too much television, surfing chat rooms on the Internet, chatting on the phone or in some other unsupportive way. The trouble is that although this temporarily alleviates the pain, life will continually put them back in this "unconquerable" situation. If they continue to retreat into their holes, they live a life full of fear and disappointment. Sometimes, however, the pain builds up to a breaking point, requiring them to immediately *move the rock* out of necessity to stay alive.

The tragic irony of this vicious cycle is that if you stand tall in the face of your fears, confronting the source of your pain directly, your life dramatically changes. Why? Because, after you *move the rock* you can do it again without fearing 'it can't be done'. Only then, can you experience true freedom and develop the strength and power to make things happen on a daily basis.

When Caught Between a Rock and a Hard Place

1. Move the rock, or
2. Blow through the hard place

Oh, I almost forgot...you're going to be back between that rock and hard place again. It will be a tighter spot with absolutely no light peering through, more daunting than before. You may even muster up the strength to break through like last time. Only this time, pushing against the rock only drains you. What then? Once again, get excited. You are about to experience a shift in who you are as you display your invincible courage.

To consistently *create the impossible*, tap into that infinite reservoir of courage and passion continually flowing within you. Stand tall as if a red cape is flowing behind you. Breathe deeply as you feel life's energy surge through your body. Be strong, stronger than you ever thought possible. Then attack your fear head on, knowing you will find a way to move forward—you always do.

Next, *smash the rock. Obliterate the hard place.* When you do, you will once again experience a level of freedom and joy that you cannot imagine. You become a person of extraordinary power, someone who is respected, and someone who makes things happen, a *Creator of the Impossible.*

Conquering Impossible Challenges

The Art of Failure

*Far better it is to dare mighty things, to win glorious triumphs,
even though checkered by failure, than to rank with those poor
spirits who neither enjoy much nor suffer much, because they
live in the gray twilight that knows neither victory nor defeat.*
—Theodore Roosevelt

There is an art form that has gone unnoticed throughout
history. Within the mysteries of this lost art lie treasures of
prosperity and fulfillment. Those few individuals who have
learned the secrets of this art have prospered regardless of
their past socio-economic conditions or any other seemingly
insurmountable obstacles.

The *art of failure*. It is a critical skill you must learn and
master if you are to excel in your *Journey to the Impossible*.
The process of failure, of getting knocked on your butt—is
the key to unlocking the secrets of success in any endeavor.
The true *art of failure* is in understanding that in the *creation*

process, bumps, snags, trips, blocks, downturns, mistakes, oopses, failures, defeats, injustices, and so on, are just stops along the way to getting what we want.

So-called "failures" are nothing to fear and in adopting the *art of failure*, you learn to actually embrace the process—every "failure" offers great insight and opens new doors of opportunity. *Failure is a critical element to achievement.* When you align yourself with your desires, your failures usually denote progress.

Practitioners of this *art* also know that "failing" is important for another reason. If you don't put yourself in the position to fail by trying new and unfamiliar things, the life you want will always remain out of reach. Why? Because to get what we want, we must grow, and growth requires risk. These practitioners also understand the value of failing quickly by simply going for it—they fail rapidly in order to create what they want. And the end result is always astounding.

One last thought on failure—the concept of quitting after things don't go your way must be a foreign concept to those on the *Journey*. You must keep changing your approach when something is not working out but...give up? Uh uh, not happening.

When All Else Fails

*The big question is whether you are going to be
able to say a hearty "yes" to your adventure.*
—Joseph Campbell

Who are you kidding? We both know this can't be the case. When all else fails, try something else. As an **Impossibility Seeker**, it is your responsibility never to accept defeat, to uncover solutions when everyone else says it's "impossible." In fact, when you hear someone say, "we've tried everything," your eyes should widen, because you are being called into the batter's box. *In life, there are infinite at-bats, so keep swinging.*

Many people think life's rules are like baseball—three strikes and you're out. They find something that they want, and they try several different things that don't work. So they give up. I'm probably being generous since many people only try one or two different strategies. (Can you imagine baseball with this rule: One strike and you're out?

The game would certainly be over much quicker.)

The secret to the *Journey* is simple: When you are committed, you will find a way. Understand that many things will not work, but you will press forward until you make that magical discovery you seek. It's never a question of "if," only a question of "when." Failure is not an option because "failure" just means you get another at-bat. Aim for the bleachers and swing away.

When "all else fails," try something else.
Life gives us infinite at-bats, so keep swinging.

Pain: A Driving Force

Several years ago, I was caught in one of those precarious positions. I was being forced to leave the place I was living. I was in deep debt, I had no source of income, and my young business had lost momentum. My stress was becoming overwhelming. I felt the pressure and helplessness of not knowing what to do. I felt embarrassed and ashamed at my predicament. I was hurting, afraid, and in pain. I didn't know where to turn or what to do.

You know the great thing about all this? The whole situation was just too painful. That's right, the situation was completely unbearable. I hated feeling totally out of control. The pain was so great that it created a major shift in my emotional state—I reached a turning point. I went from being afraid to angry to determined to make immediate changes in my life. *That pain became my driving force*. And when that happened, my life changed forever. I was back in the driver's seat.

Here's the amazing part: Before I even took the first action, I felt dramatically different. I felt stronger, more energized, more focused. I broke the bonds of my self-encapsulated cell and achieved mental clarity and strength in the process.

The resources are within you to create the change you want, but only if you keep your focus on what you want.

With my renewed mental clarity, my personal resources exploded in a million directions. I began to formulate strategies for conquering each challenge and thinking of different resources that I had but was not using.

I immediately began developing a plan for creating income to eradicate my debt and pay rent as well. I found late night temping and contract work that paid well and gave me the freedom to work on my projects, such as starting my consulting company and developing more effective business strategies, during the day. I got more excited by the minute. Each step in the process was a small victory, which led to much larger victories. But that wasn't what mattered. I had already won—I was out of my *hole*. I was back in control of my life and building momentum.

We often wait until the pain is unbearable to make the shift. We wait until our weight reaches astronomical levels, our finances are completely embarrassing, and our relationships are nearly unsalvageable. Why? We often need something unbearably painful driving us in order to cultivate an unstoppable emotional state within ourselves.

In your *Journey to the Impossible*, clarify what you want and use all problems, challenges, and pain as driving forces to help you get where you want to go.

The Human Catapult

Pain can be an incredible ally that propels you forward, helping you create the life you deserve. Think of pain as a human catapult. You want to propel over the wall to meet your destiny and all the wonderful treasures of life, but the catapult takes you back first, away from the direction of your destiny. When the catapult's tension is at its maximum, it releases you. Then you soar free and clear the wall.

Climbing the Wall

In three words I can sum up everything
I've learned about life. It goes on.
—Robert Frost

Now, imagine you are living your vision, tapped into your fire, rockin' and rollin'. You are working overtime on your job to save extra money to help create your empire. Then you come home and really bear down, working another six hours on your project, building the foundation for your extraordinary lifestyle. You're thriving, although sleep deprived, because you know you're planting invaluable seeds that will grow into your extraordinary future. In every sense of the term, you are **Creating the Impossible**. But then you hit a wall.

Your unbridled enthusiasm and energy begin to wane, you begin to lose steam, and your momentum falters. Your environment throws up a huge 15-foot brick wall that goes on forever. You are working so hard to *conquer the unthinkable*, and you are just not seeing any visible results to warrant such a tenacious pursuit. You have hit a *wall*. You may even begin to question what you are doing, wondering if your quest is worth the time and energy. A downward spiral envelops you.

This *wall* marks a critically important time in your life. The decisions you make here and, consequently, the actions you take will ultimately determine your destiny, your quality of life, and your ability to *create* now and forever.

You must do only one *thing* when you hit this wall. The power of this one *thing* is difficult to explain in words. The reason why the majority of people on this planet do not *Journey to the Impossible* is because they never do this one *thing*.

The one *thing* you must do when you hit a *wall* is to *take one more action*! When you're tired, when you feel you've given all you got, when you just can't will yourself to lunge forward—you must find within yourself the strength to *take one more action toward your vision*.

One way to do this is to reconnect with your *fire* and your passion, clarifying why you are on this *Journey* in the first place. Close your eyes and project forward in your mind, visualizing the creation and manifestation of your wants and desires. Stay in this place for as long as you need. Breathe. Smile. Feel the pain and lethargy just melt away.

Feel a surge of energy, revitalizing and electrifying your body, giving you the strength and power to move forward with even greater tenacity. Put on some music, shout out loud, jump up and down, go for a run—do whatever it takes to recharge. And then plunge forward.

Remember, you're a *Creator,* an *Impossibility Seeker*— a warrior of everyday life who will not be denied. You will find a way.

Top athletes play at full capacity throughout any competition, and when they are out of energy, they find a way to go another round. Most of us, however, don't have this reaction when we run out of steam. Out of fear, we think that we're tapped out. After all, sometimes it's just easier to let the game go. To drop out. To just say, "I've had enough." But you can't create anything if you just "let it go." *Turn up the heat!*

Also, acknowledge all your efforts thus far—don't beat yourself up for hitting a *wall.* This obstacle poses just another challenge, nothing to get discouraged about, and definitely not worth the price of getting down on yourself. There is a delicate balance between demanding a lot from yourself, setting amazingly high standards and not coming down on yourself when things don't work out the way you want.

You can create whatever you want in your life, but it's a process. The *Journey* may take longer than you want. It's a daily challenge. As soon as you tackle one obstacle, another will arise. This denotes progress—it means you're being challenged to grow and there are multiple rewards to come. Each day we must step up to the challenge of daily creation and embrace life.

Getting down on yourself regarding things you cannot control is just plain idiotic. Learn to acknowledge your *Journey*. Trust your abilities to create your vision. Stay focused on what you want, and each day do what needs to be done. When you do, you will truly live free, and you will strive to experience these emotions each and every day of your life.

The Journey Continues

Although this may be the end of this book, your *Journey* is really just beginning. In fact, the *Journey* never ends—it just keeps getting better and better.

You now have an arsenal of ideas, tools, and strategies to design a truly extraordinary life on your never-ending *Journey to the Impossible*. You have valuable tools for getting results, questions for discovering your vision and the three *laws of creation*. You have fantastic insights into how to truly live the **impossible life.** The strategies for cultivating innovation and creativity in this book can change the way you think and help you produce real magic in your own life. You have new perspectives in the areas of growth, leadership, health, wealth, and challenges to help shape your process of thinking and decision-making.

The Journey Continues

Now it's time for you to become the master architect of your own life. Design a magical adventure you can be proud of for all eternity.

Remember that when your *Journey* takes you to a wall, a mountain that appears to be insurmountable, know that something great is about to happen. Resolve to believe in your ability to master any challenge and tackle any obstacle. You are now a **Creator of the Impossible**, in fact, you always were—but now you know for certain.

I hope we will continue our *Journey* together. Maybe your story will inspire future **Creators of the Impossible**. I would enjoy hearing or reading any stories that may transpire as a result of these ideas. Please visit www.scottjeffrey.com to share your comments or email me at scott@scottjeffrey.com.

I wish you a truly wondrous adventure. May you discover what you seek, live fully, embrace each day, and make the world a better place.

Happy Journeys!
–Scott Jeffrey

Happy Journeys!

Resource Guide

Achieving Impossible Results

Allen, James. *As a Man Thinketh*. 1904.

Buckingham, Marcus and Curt Coffman. *First, Break All the Rules*. New York: Simon & Schuster, 1999.

Covey, Stephen R. *The Seven Habits of Highly Effective People*. New York: Simon & Schuster, 1989.

Danforth, William H. *I Dare You*. St. Louis: The American Youth Foundation, 1967.

Goonies. Director Richard Donner. With Sean Astin. Warner Bros, 1985.

Johnson, Crockett. *Harold and the Purple Crayon*. New York: Harper & Row, 1955.

Robbins, Anthony. *The Time of Your Life: More Time for What Really Matters to You*. San Diego: Robbins Research International, 1998.

Robbins, Anthony. *Unlimited Power*. New York: Ballantine Books, 1986.

Vogler, Christopher. *The Writer's Journey: Mythic Structure for Writers*. Studio City: Michael Wiese Productions, 1998.

Mastering Impossible Living

Chopra, Deepak. *The Seven Spiritual Laws of Success*. San Rafael: Amber-Allen Publishing and New World Library, 1994.

Chopra, Deepak. *The Way of the Wizard*. New York: Harmony Books, 1995.

Coelho, Paulo. *The Alchemist*. Great Britain: Harper Collins

Publishers, 1988.

Mandino, Og. *The Greatest Salesman in the World*. New York: Bantam Books, 1968.

Millman, Dan. *Sacred Journeys of the Peaceful Warrior*. Tiburon: H J Kramer, 1991.

Millman, Dan. *The Life You Were Born to Live*. Tiburon, CA: H J Kramer, 1993.

Millman, Dan. *The Way of the Peaceful Warrior*. Tiburon, CA: H J Kramer, 1984.

Quindlen, Anna. *A Short Guide to a Happy Life*. New York: Random, 2000.

Seligman, Martin. *Learned Optimism*. New York: Pocket Books, 1990.

Star Wars: Episode V – The Empire Strikes Back. Director Irvin Kershner. Story, George Lucas. With Mark Hamill, Harrison Ford and Carrie Fisher. 20th Century Fox Film, 1980.

Cultivating Impossible Creativity

Abbott, Edwin A. *Flatland: A Romance of Many Dimensions*. New York: Dover Publishing, 1992.

Adams, Douglas. *The Hitcher's Guide to the Galaxy*. New York: Pocket Books, 1979.

Buzan, Tony. *The Mind Map Book*. New York: Penguin Books, 1996.

Gelb, Michael. *How to Think Like Leonardo da Vinci*. New York: Delacourte Press, 1998.

Kao, John. *Jamming*. New York: Harper Collins Publishers, 1996.

Kawasaki, Guy and Michele Moreno. *Rules for Revolutionaries*. New York: Harper Collins Publishers, 1998.

Oech, Roger von. *A Whack on the Side of the Head*. Menlo Park: CreativeThink, 1983.

Shekerjian, Denise. *Uncommon Genius: How Great Ideas are Born.* New York: Penguin Group, 1990.

Strong, Morgan. "Richard Branson: The ICON Profile." ICON Dec. 1998: 88-99.

Ueland, Brenda. *If You Want to Write: A Book about Art, Independence and Spirit.* Saint Paul: Graywolf Press,1987.

Williams, Roy H. *The Wizard of Ads: Turning Words into Magic and Dreamers into Millionaires.* Austin: Bard Press, 1998.

Committing to Impossible Growth

Adler, Mortimer J, and Charles Van Doren. *How to Read a Book.* New York: Simon & Schuster, 1972.

Lee, Bruce. *Tao of Jeet Kune Do.* Santa Clarita: Ohara Publications, 1975.

McGraw, Phillip C. *Life Strategies Workbook.* New York: Hyperion, 2000.

Millman, Dan. *No Ordinary Moments: A Peaceful Warrior's Guide to Daily Life.* Tiburon, CA: H J Kramer, 1992.

Scheele, Paul R. *Natural Brilliance.* Wayzata, MN: Learning Strategies Corporation, 2000.

Scheele, Paul R. *The PhotoReading Whole Mind System.* Wayzata, MN: Learning Strategies Corporation, 1997.

Schur, Norman. *1000 Most Important Words.* New York: Ballantine Books, 1982.

Wilkinson, Bruce. *The Prayer of Jabez.* Sisters, OR: Multnomah Publishers, 2000.

Living Impossible Leadership

Blanchard, Kenneth, and Spencer Johnson. *The One-Minute Manager.* New York: Berkley Books, 1981.

Carnegie, Dale. *How to Win Friends and Influence People.*

New York: Simon & Schuster, 1981.

Carnegie, Dale. *The Quick and Easy Way to Effective Speaking*. Garden City: Dale Carnegie & Associates, 1962.

Cialdini, Robert B. Influence: *The Psychology of Persuasion*. New York: William Morrow and Company, 1993.

Johnson, Spencer. *Who Moved My Cheese?* New York: G.P. Putnam's Sons, 1998.

Maxwell, John and Jim Dornan. *Becoming a Person of Influence*. Nashville: Thomas Nelson Publishers, 1997.

Maintaining Impossible Health

Aihara, Herman. *Acid and Alkaline*. Oroville, CA: George Ohsawa Macrobotic Foundation, 1986.

Batmanghelidj, Fereydoon, M.D. *Your Body's Many Cries For Water*. Vienna, VA: Global Health Solutions, 1997.

Loehr, James E., and Peter J. McLaughlin. *Mental Toughness Training Program: Commanding the Ideal Performance State at Will*. Niles, IL: Nightingale-Conant.

Millman, Dan. *Everyday Enlightenment: The Twelve Gateways to Personal Growth*. New York: Warner Books, 1998. (Peaceful Warrior Workout)

Robbins, Anthony. *Living Health: 10 Steps to Creating the Health, Vitality, and Energy You Deserve*. San Diego: The Anthony Robbins Companies, 1999.

Weil, Andrew. *Eight Weeks to Optimum Health*. New York: Alfred A. Knopf, 1997.

Creating Impossible Wealth

Chilton, David. *The Wealthy Barber*. United States: Prima Publishing, 1998.

Clason, George. *The Richest Man in Babylon*. New York:

Penguin Group, 1955.

Fisher, Mark. *The Instant Millionaire*. Novato: New World Library, 1990.

Fridson, Martin. *How to be a Billionaire*. New York: John Wiley & Sons, Inc, 2000.

Getty, J. Paul. *How to be Rich*. New York: Jove Books, 1965.

Hill, Napoleon. *Think and Grow Rich*. New York: Fawcett Crest, 1960.

Kiyosaki, Robert T and Sharon L Lechter. *Rich Dad, Poor Dad*. New York: Warner Books, 1998.

Pilzer, Paul Zane. *God Wants you to be Rich*. New York: Simon & Schuster, 1995.

Stanley, Thomas and William Danko. *The Millionaire Next Door*. Atlanta: Longstreet Press, 1996.

Developing Impossible Relationships

Bonnstetter, Bill J., Judy I. Suiter, and Randy J. Widrick. *The Universal DISC Language: A Reference Manual*. Target Training International, 1993.

Chapman, Gary. *The Five Love Languages*. Chicago: Northfield Publishing, 1995.

Deida, David. *The Way of the Superior Man*. Austin: Plexus, 1997.

Hesse, Hermann. Siddhartha. New York: MJK Books, 1951.

Keeping the Faith. Dir. Ed Norton. With Ben Stiller, Ed Norton, and Jenna Elfman. Buena Vista and Touchstone Pictures, 2000.

Conquering Impossible Challenges

Andrews, Andy. *Go For It! Series*. Franklin, TN: Dalmatian Press, 2002. (An outstanding children's book series on overcoming obstacles and challenges.)

Andrews, Andy. *Storms of Perfection: in their own words.* Nashville: Lightning Crown Publishers, 1992.

Andrews, Andy. *Storms of Perfection 2: letters from the heart.* Nashville: Lightning Crown Publishers, 1994.

Andrews, Andy. *Storms of Perfection 3: a pathway to personal achievement.* Nashville: Lightning Crown Publishers, 1996.

Andrews, Andy. *Storms of Perfection 4: letters from the past.* Nashville: Lightning Crown Publishers, 1997.

Carnegie, Dale. *How to Stop Worrying and Start Living.* New York: Pocket Books, 1984.

Frankl, Viktor E. *Man's Search For Meaning.* New York: Pocket Books, 1984.

Hoosiers. Director David Anspaugh. With Gene Hackman and Dennis Hopper. Orion Pictures, 1986.

Mansfield, Stephen. *Never Give In: The Extraordinary Character of Winston Churchill.* Elkton: Highland Books, 1995.

Rudy. Director David Anspaugh. With Sean Astin and Jon Favreau. Sony and Tristar Pictures, 1993.

Wilber, Ken. *Grace and Grit.* Boston: Shambhala Publications, 2001.

About the Author

SCOTT JEFFREY coaches entrepreneurs, CEOs, entertainers, and leaders in all areas of life toward achieving better results in less time with greater fulfillment. Scott is the master strategist behind The Scott Jeffrey Companies, a world-class strategic coaching enterprise. For nearly ten years, Scott has passionately pursued effective solutions and revolutionary strategies in the areas of business and human development. His personal entrepreneurial experiences in entertainment, new media, and financial services led him to develop strategic planning, marketing, and business development principles that would consistently yield incredible results. Scott's innovative, strategic thinking has helped in the development of over two-dozen enterprises in different stages of growth. He has written numerous articles and conducts various seminars on performance strategies, enterprise development, and personal achievement. Scott graduated with a bachelor of arts from the University of Michigan. He currently lives in New York City.

About the Companies

The Scott Jeffrey Companies is a strategic coaching enterprise designed to help individuals and businesses achieve incredible results and have greater fulfillment. The company's work is primarily with entrepreneurs and proven leaders who are already successful by modern standards, but who are constantly looking for ways to get the edge. Through dynamic workshops, one-on-one coaching, and ongoing strategic planning and development, The Scott Jeffrey Companies is committed to helping its clients take their lives and their businesses to the next level.

The Scott Jeffrey Companies also conducts *Funshops*™ for business executives, entrepreneurs, and passionate individuals. The company's newest seminar, *Dynasty in a Day*™: *Seven Powerful Steps to Creating your Empire*, has received fantastic praise for the experience and value this workshop produces.

For more information on his services,
please contact us at:

The Scott Jeffrey Companies
1173-A Second Avenue, #356
New York, NY 10021
voice/fax: (877) 201-5400
info@scottjeffrey.com

To subscribe to Scott's free e-newsletter and find out
more about his products and services, go to:

www.scottjeffrey.com